Rituals

Mandala Hearts
Adult
Coloring Book

Siobhan Maunsell

Dear Friend,
This relaxing Mandala heart Adult coloring book, was created for men and women to offer an artistic option of therapeutic art relief.

Enjoy each creating unique hearts using your favorite colored pencils, markers, pens, or crayons.

They will offer a light challenge while helping you to relax from the daily routine of life.

Yours Truly
Siobhan Maunsell

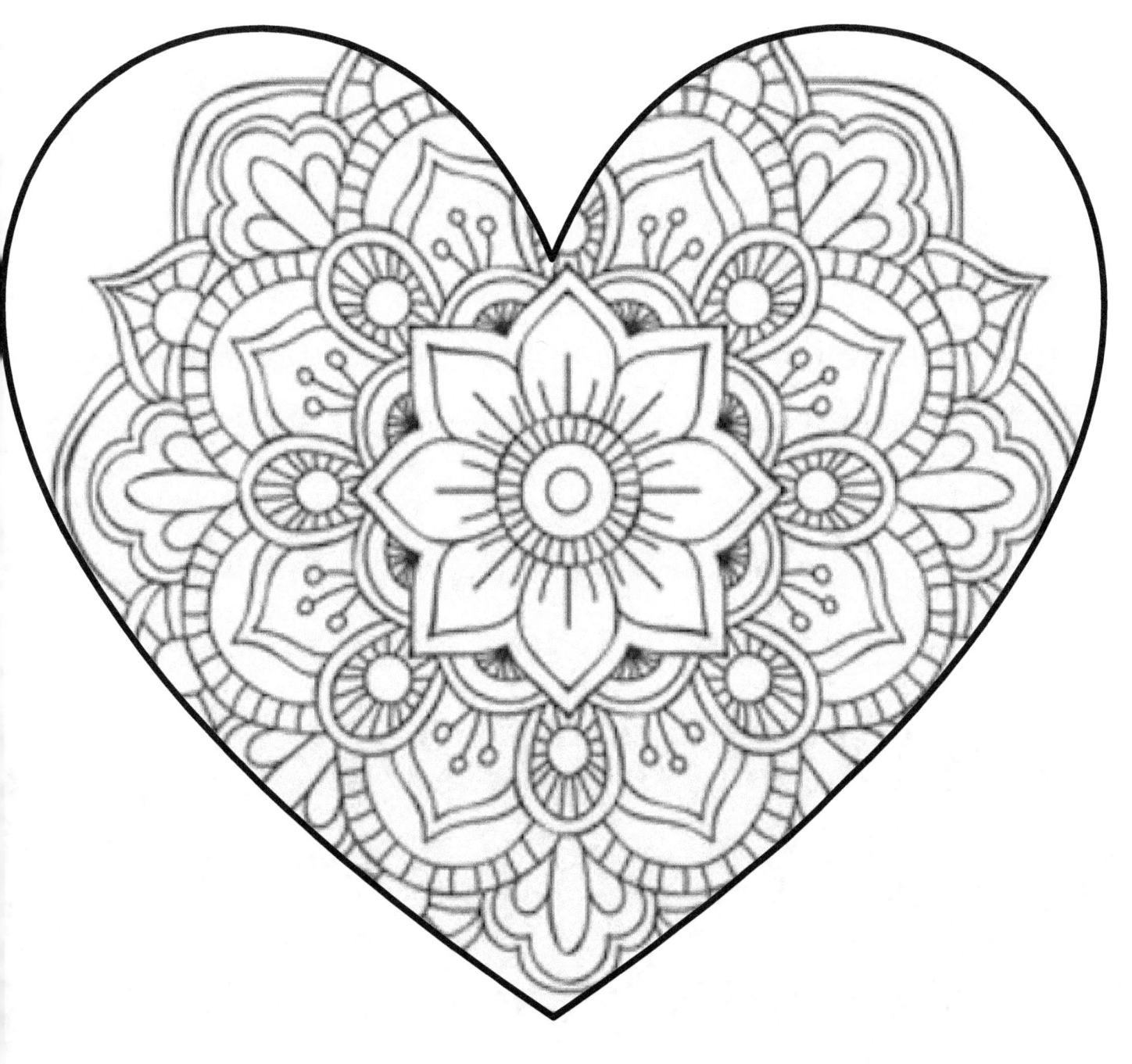

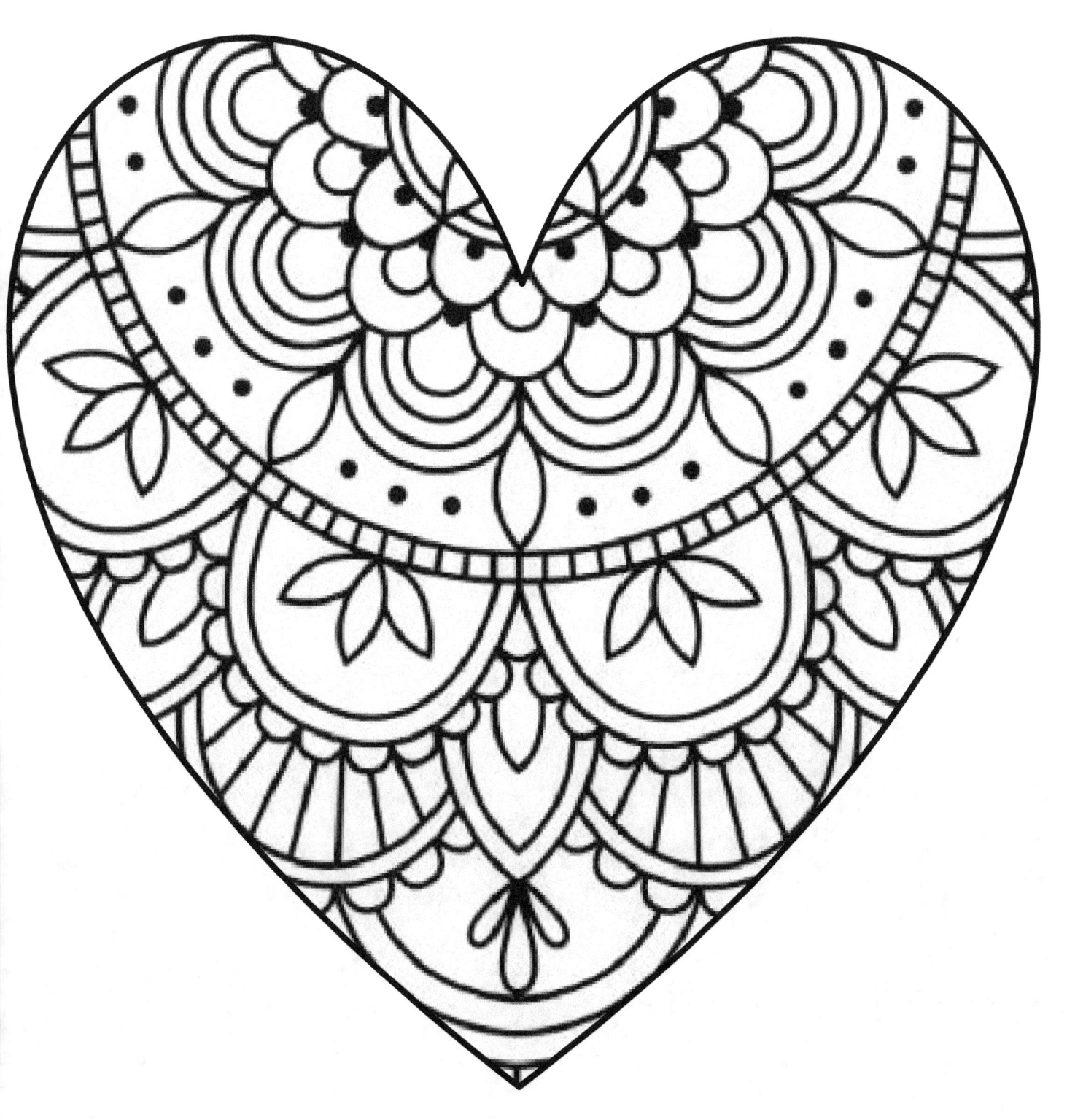

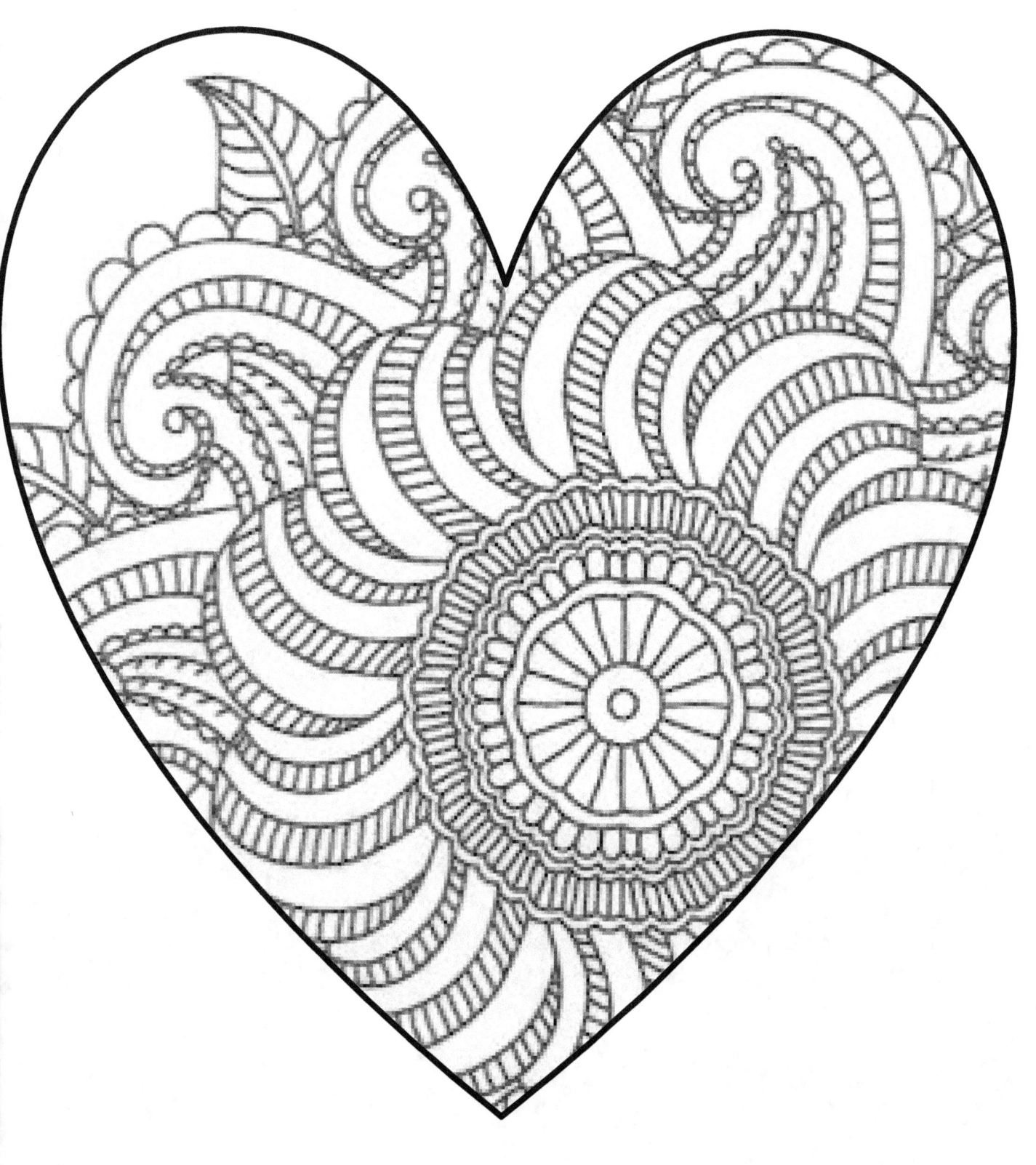

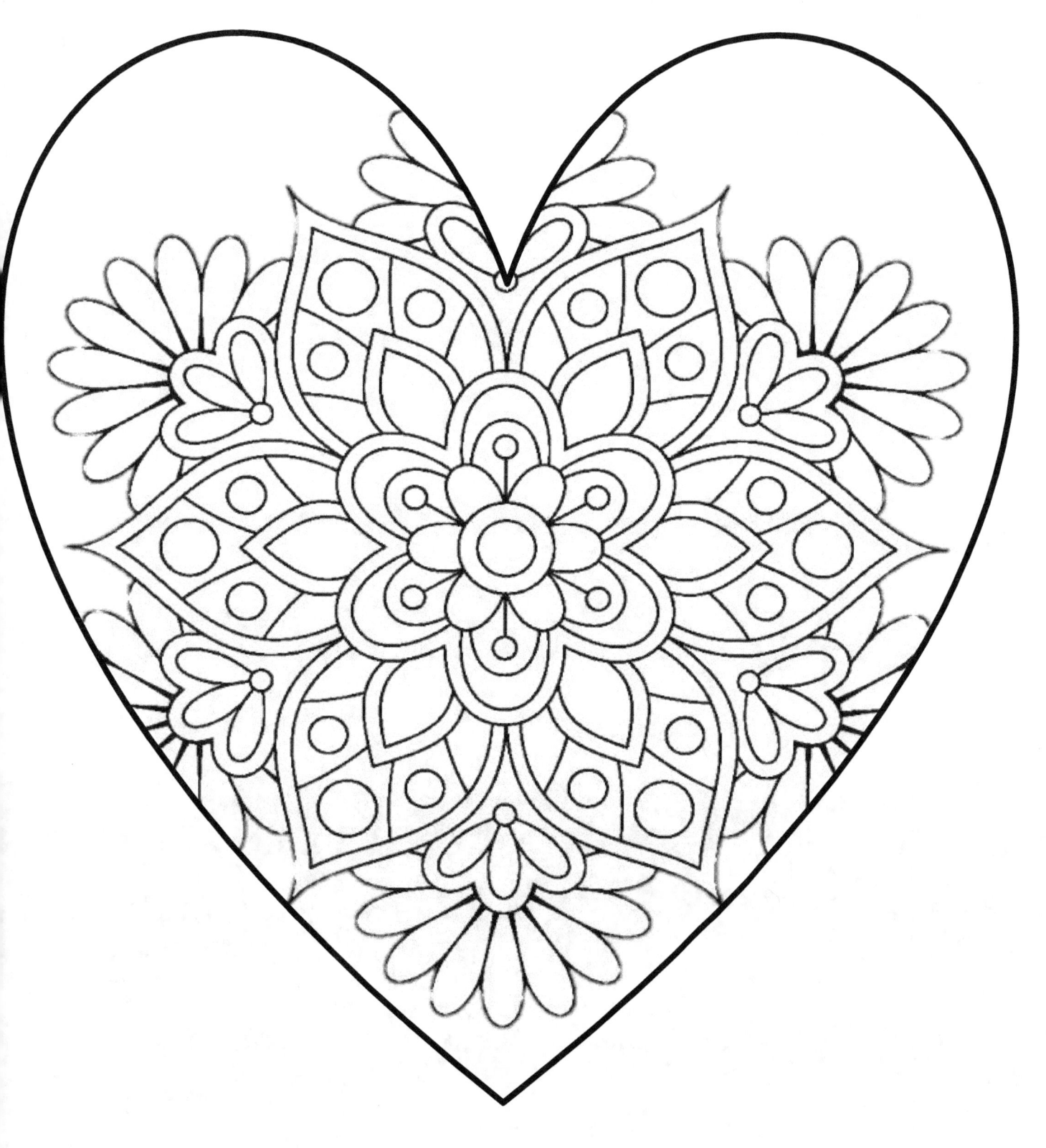

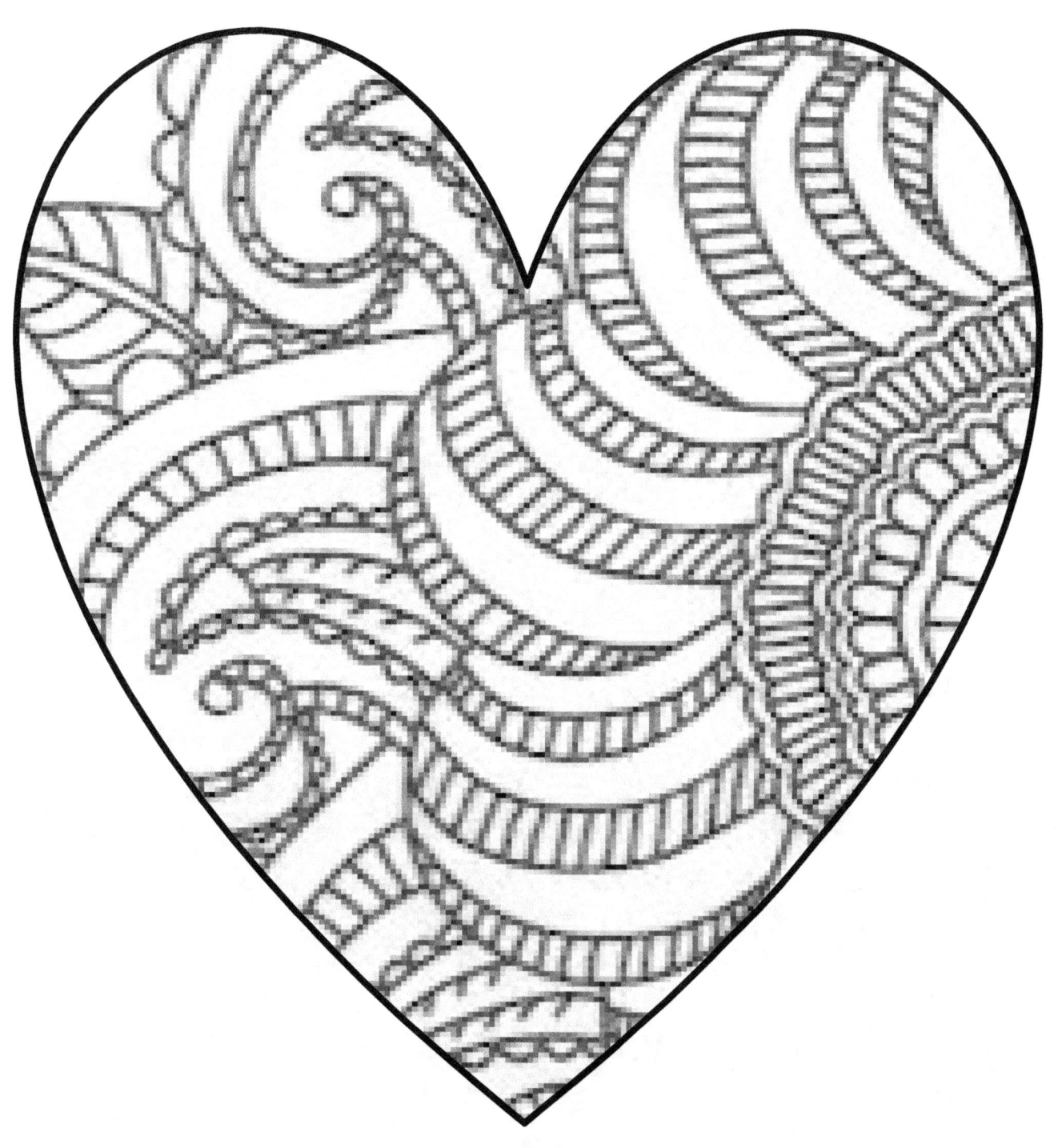

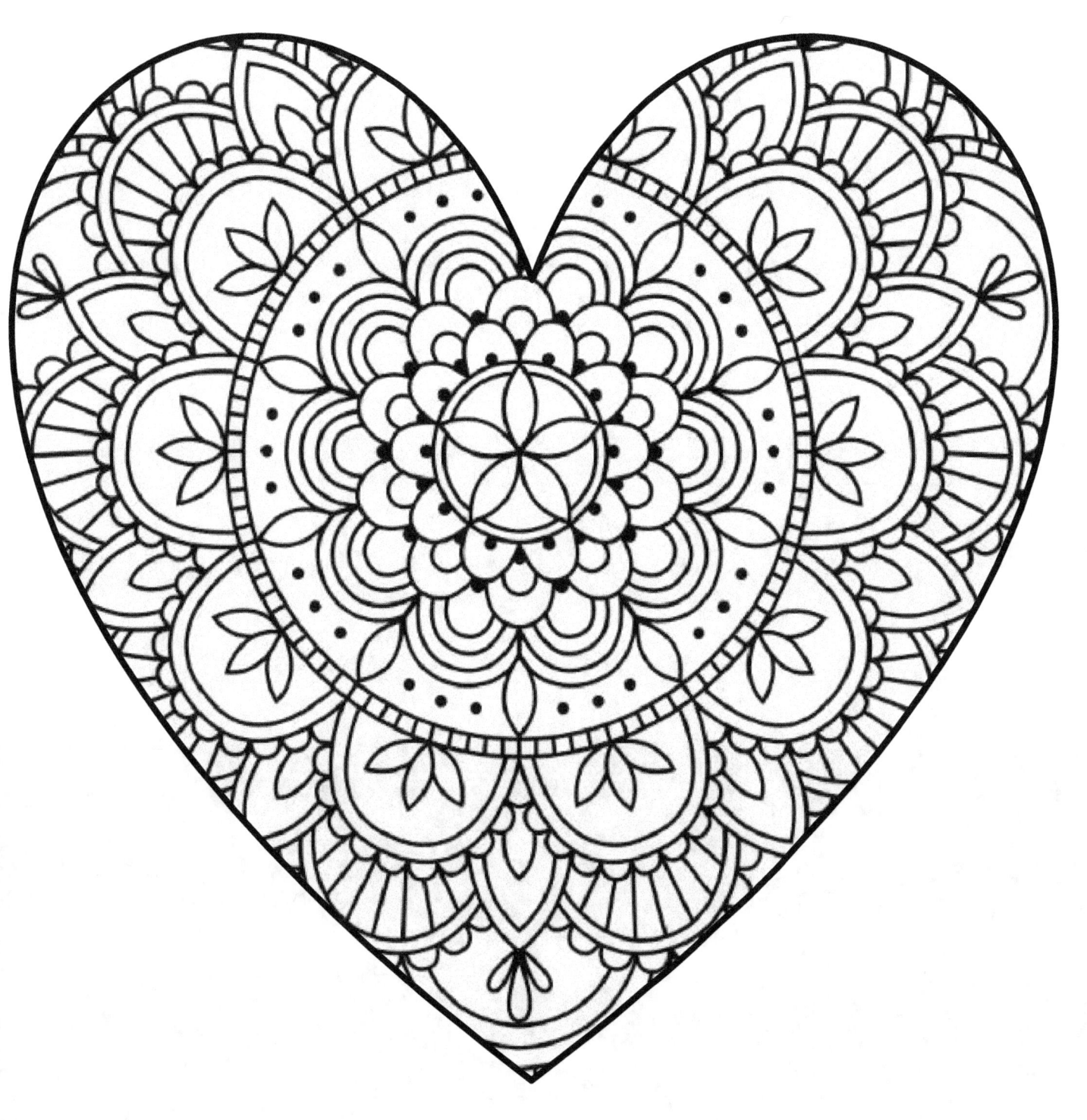

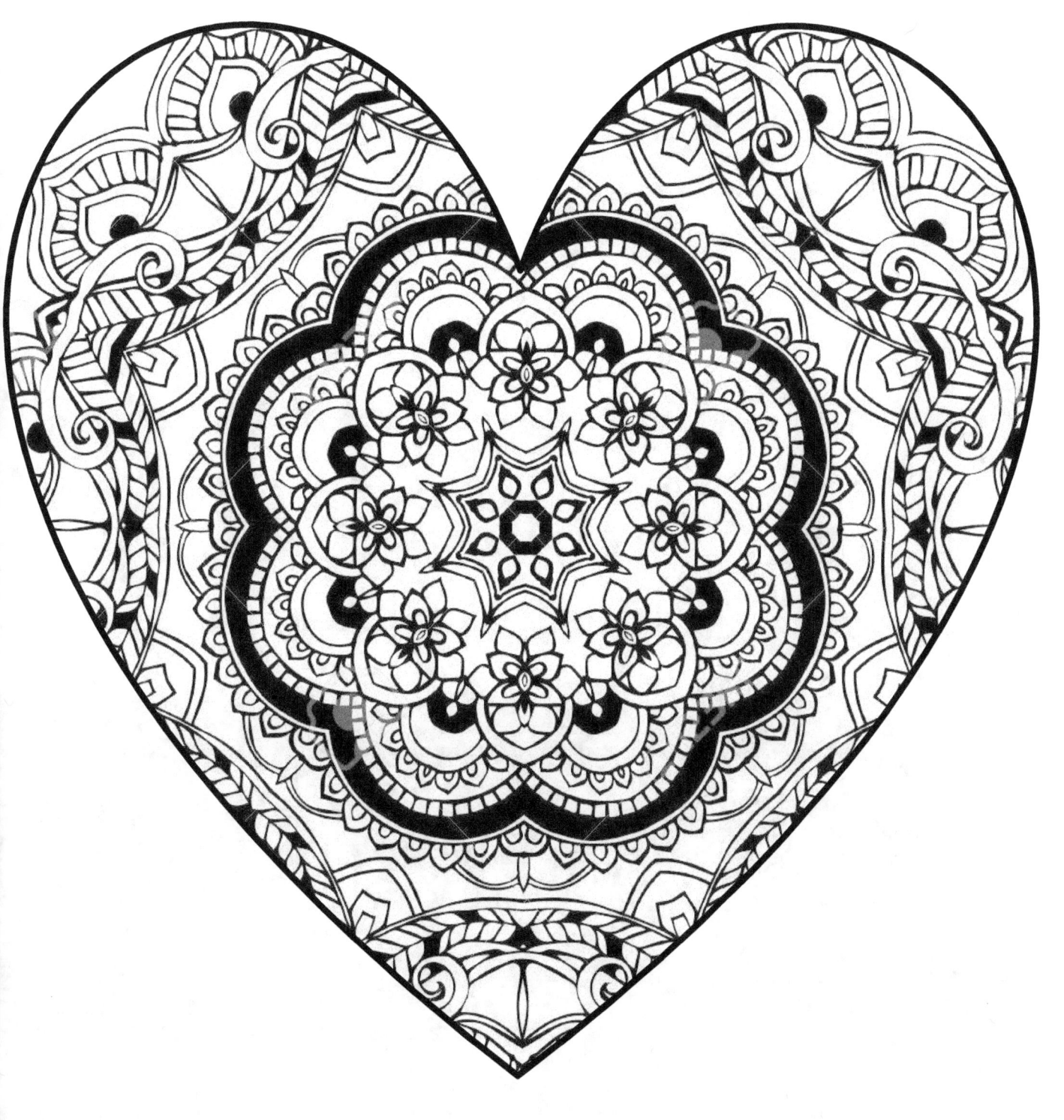

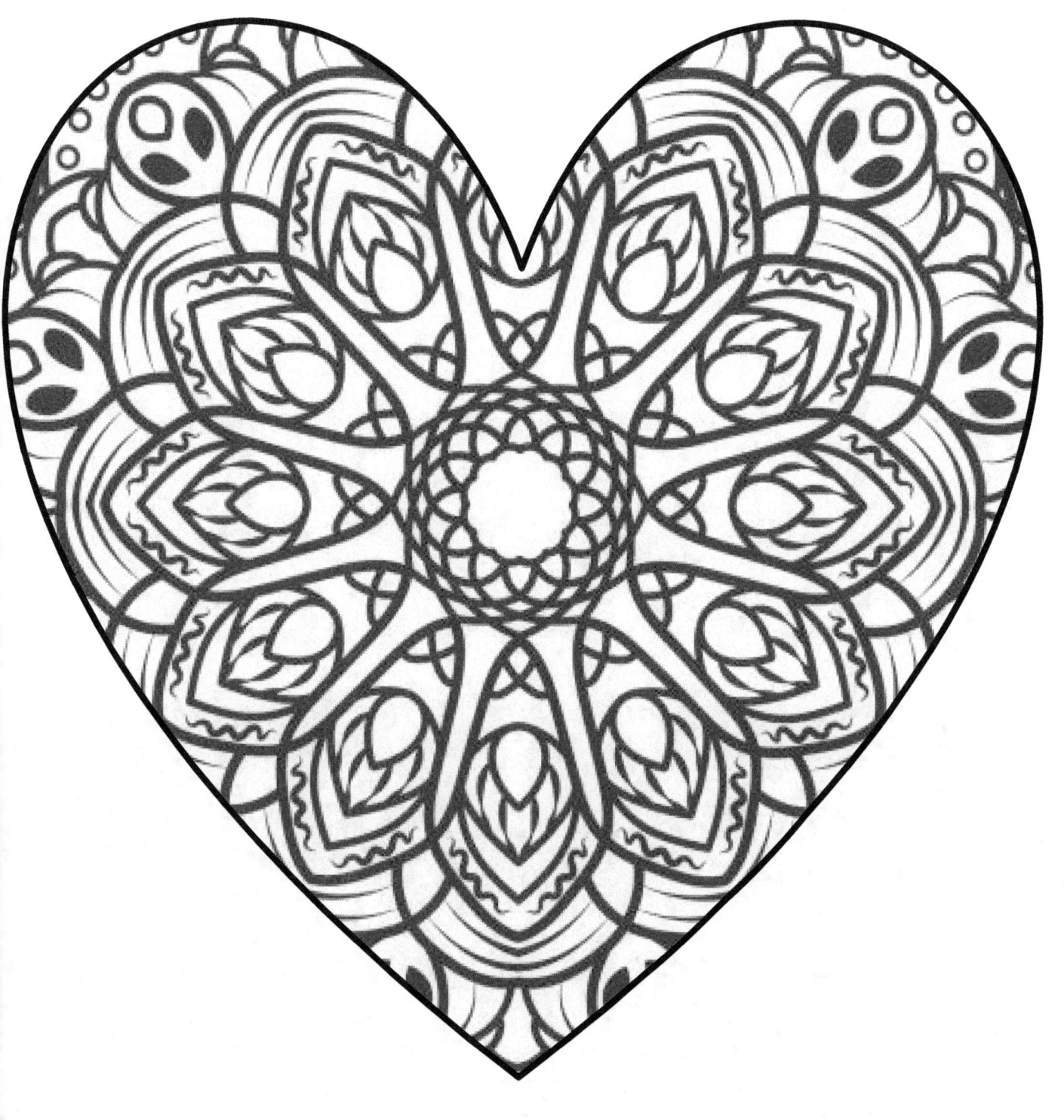

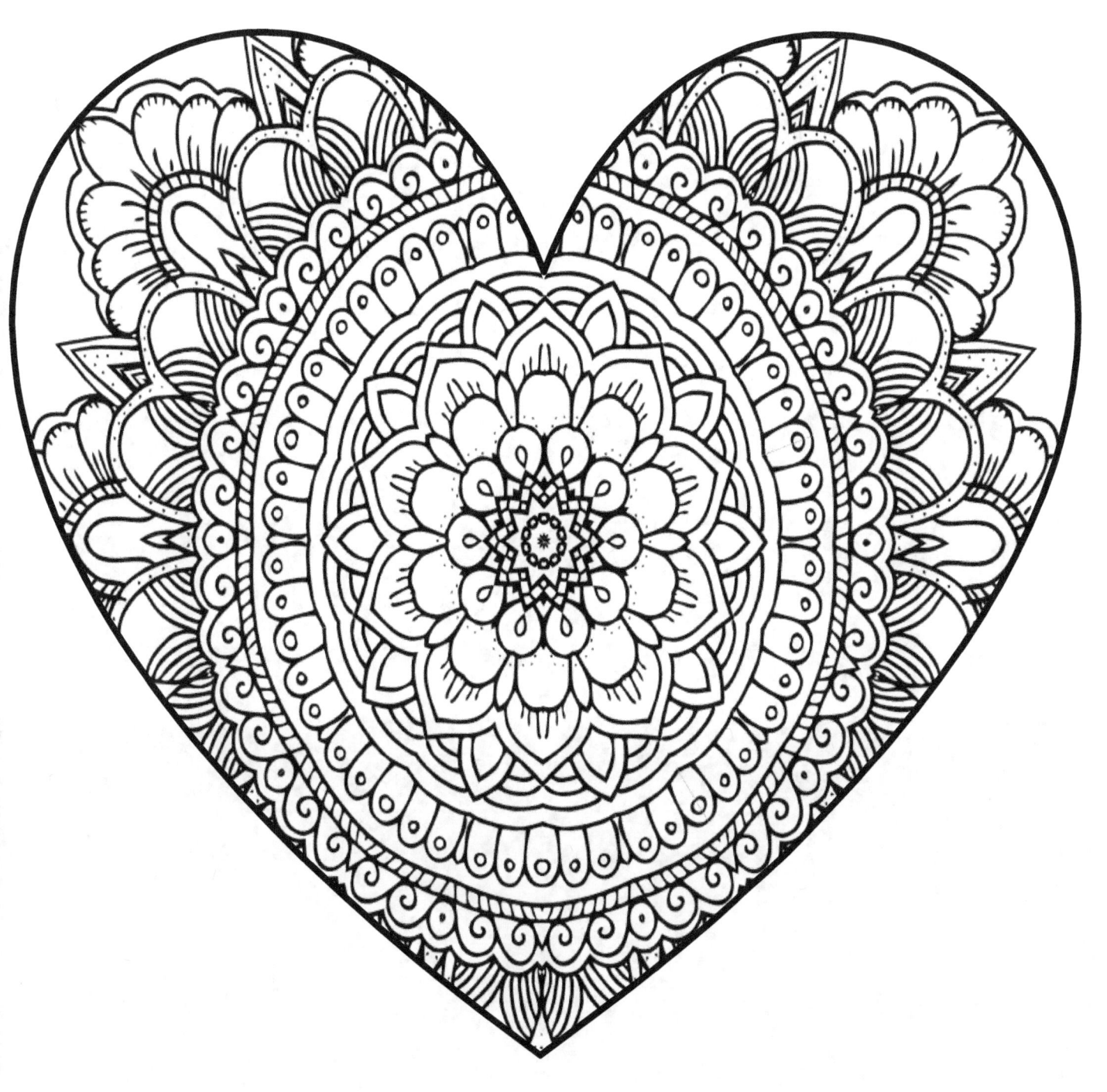

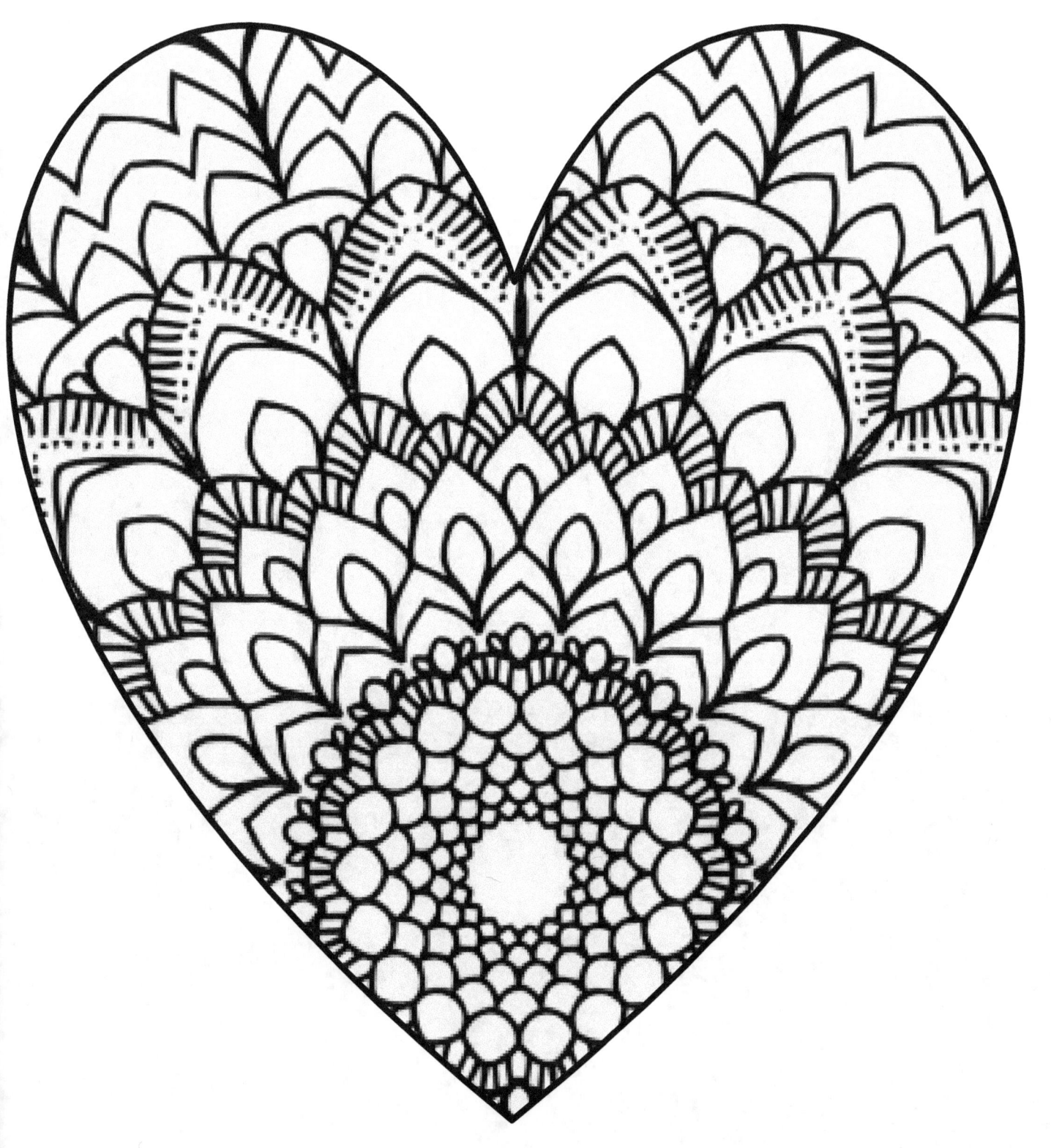

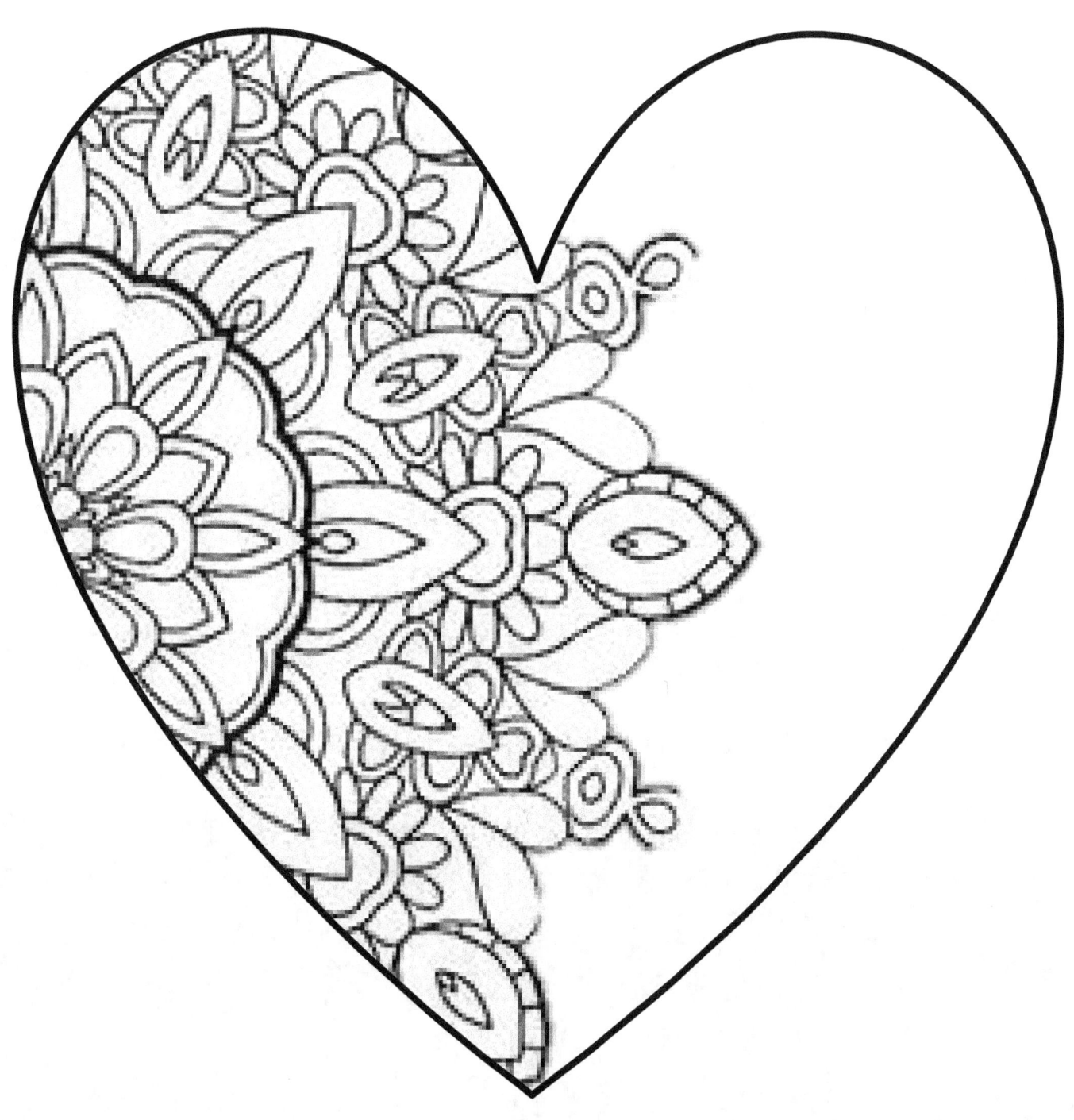

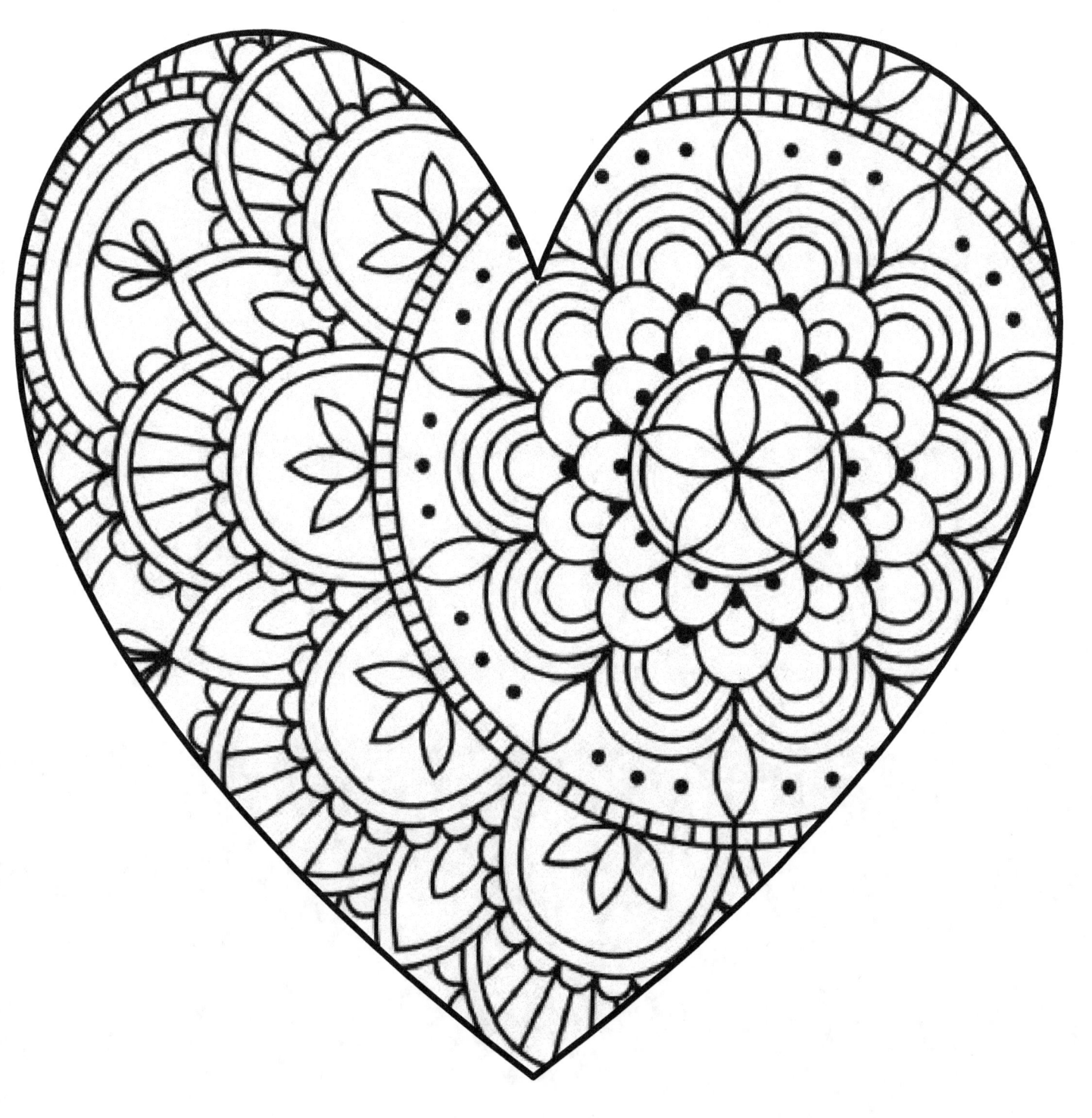

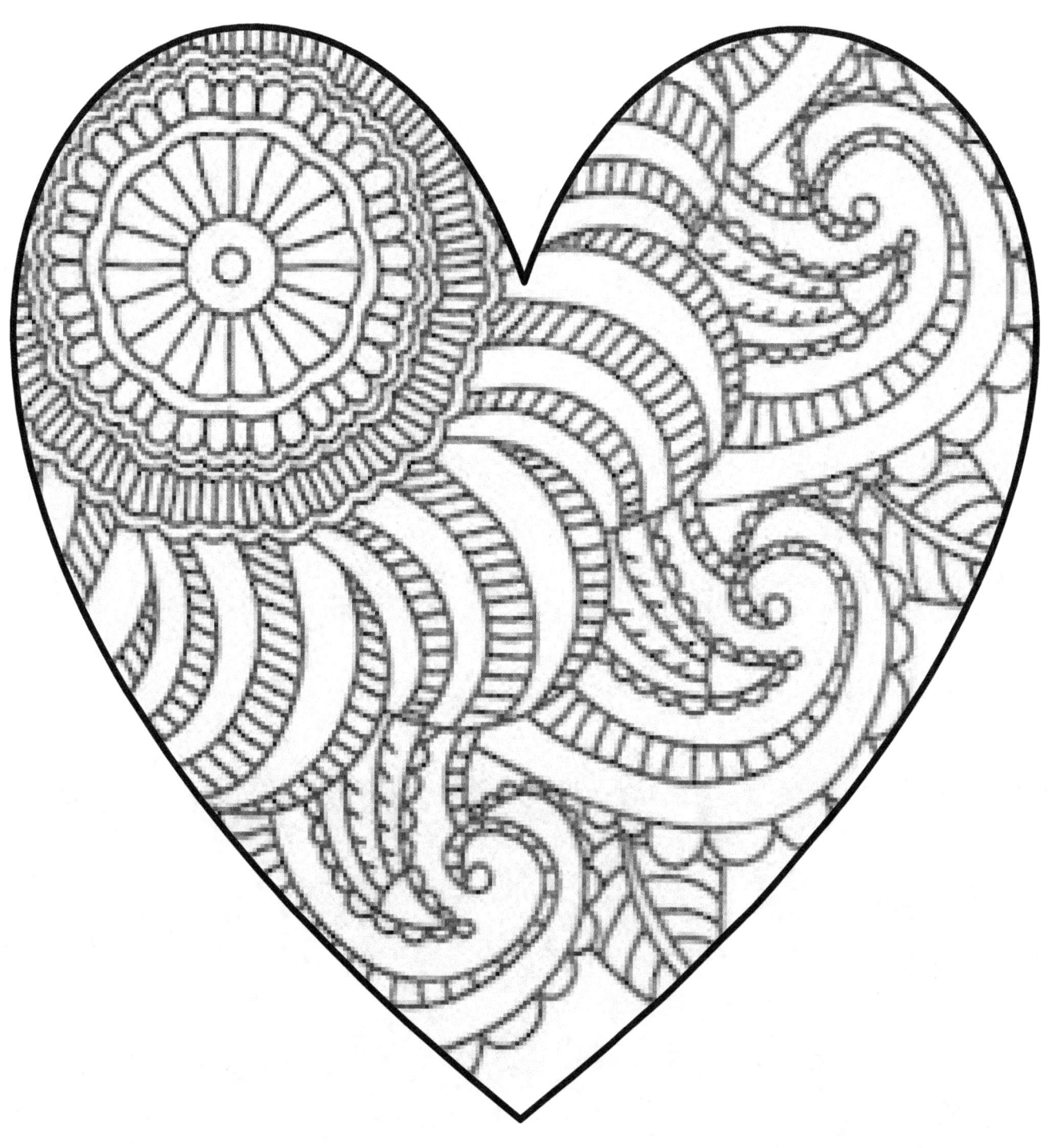

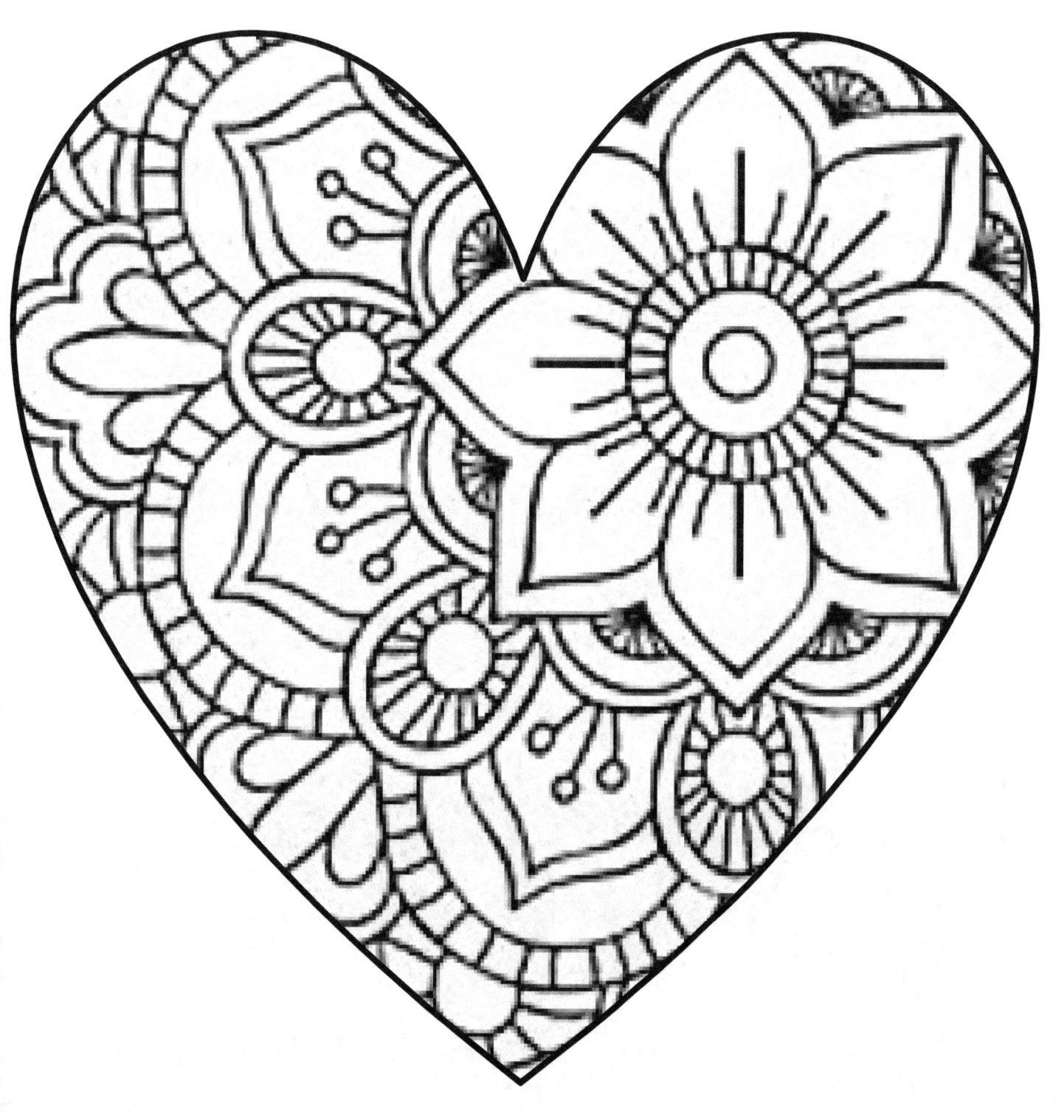

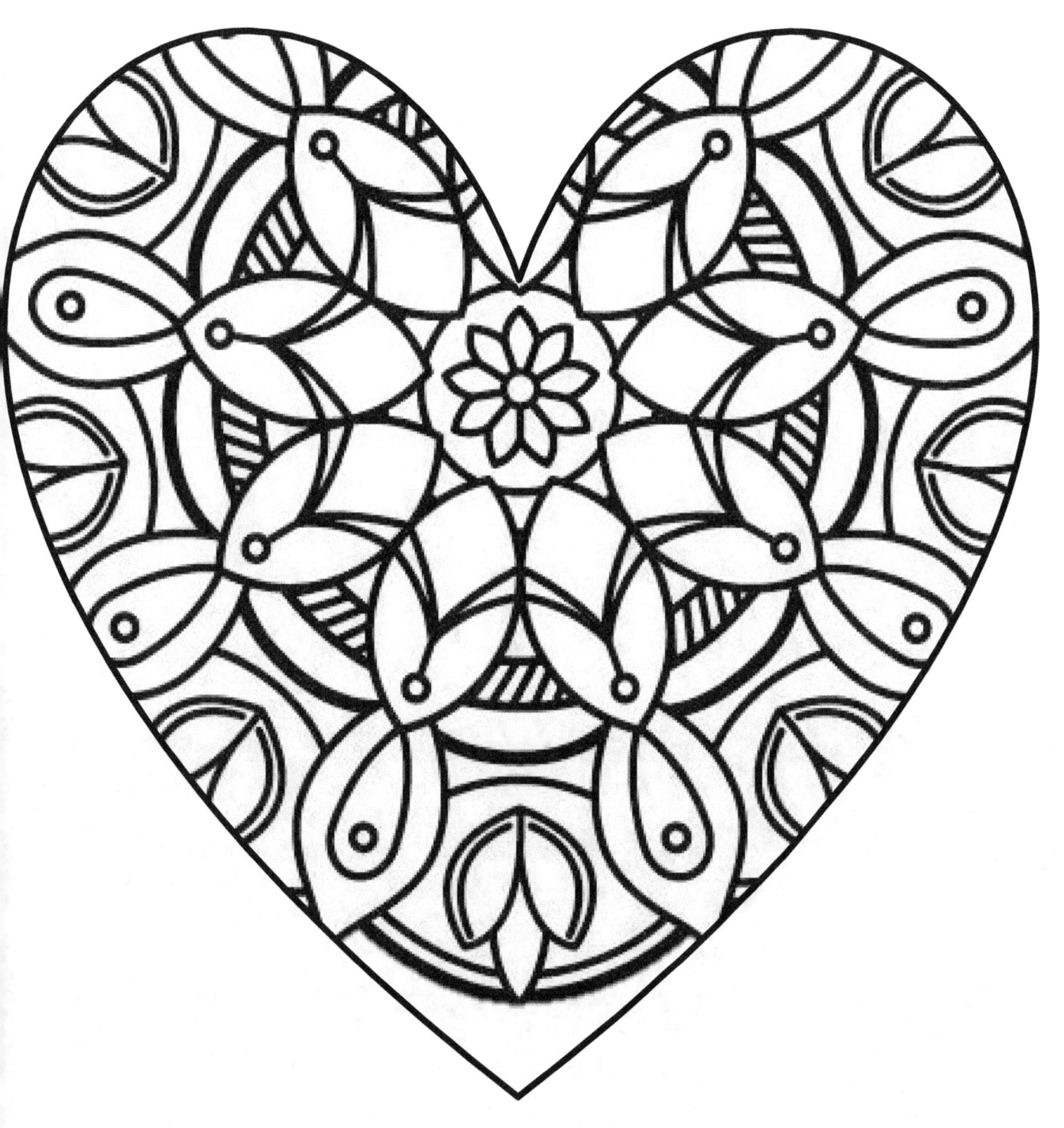

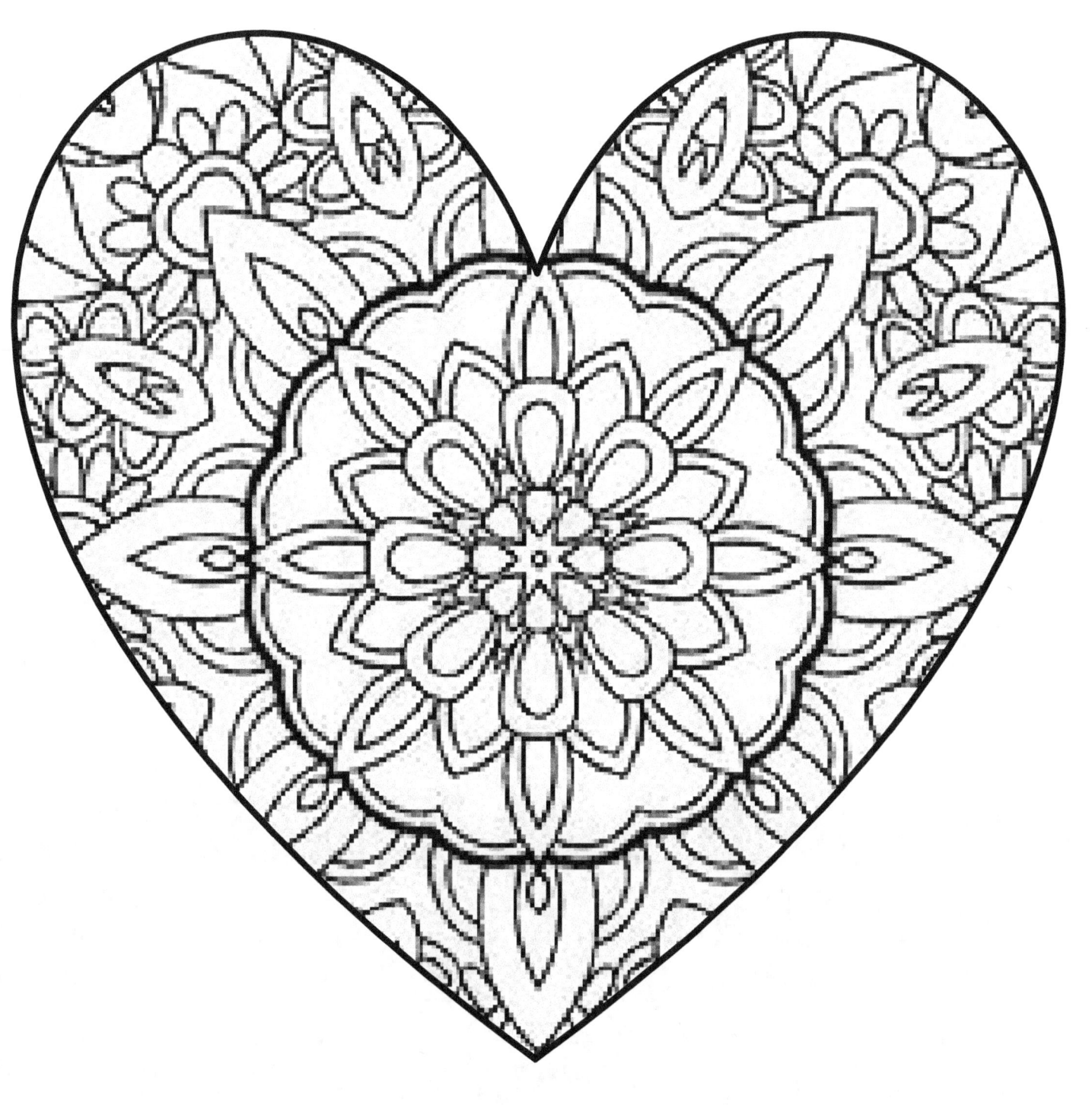

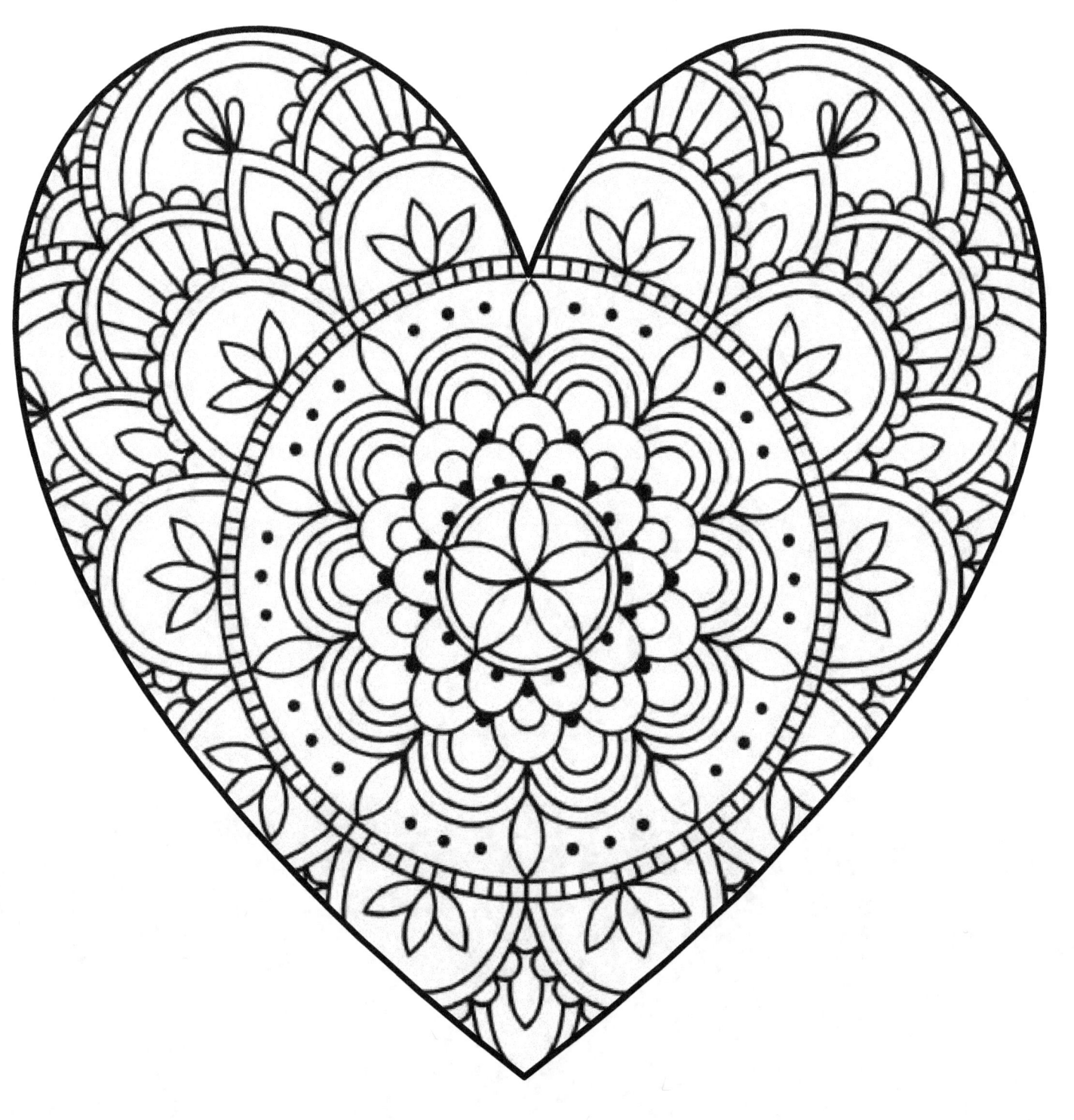

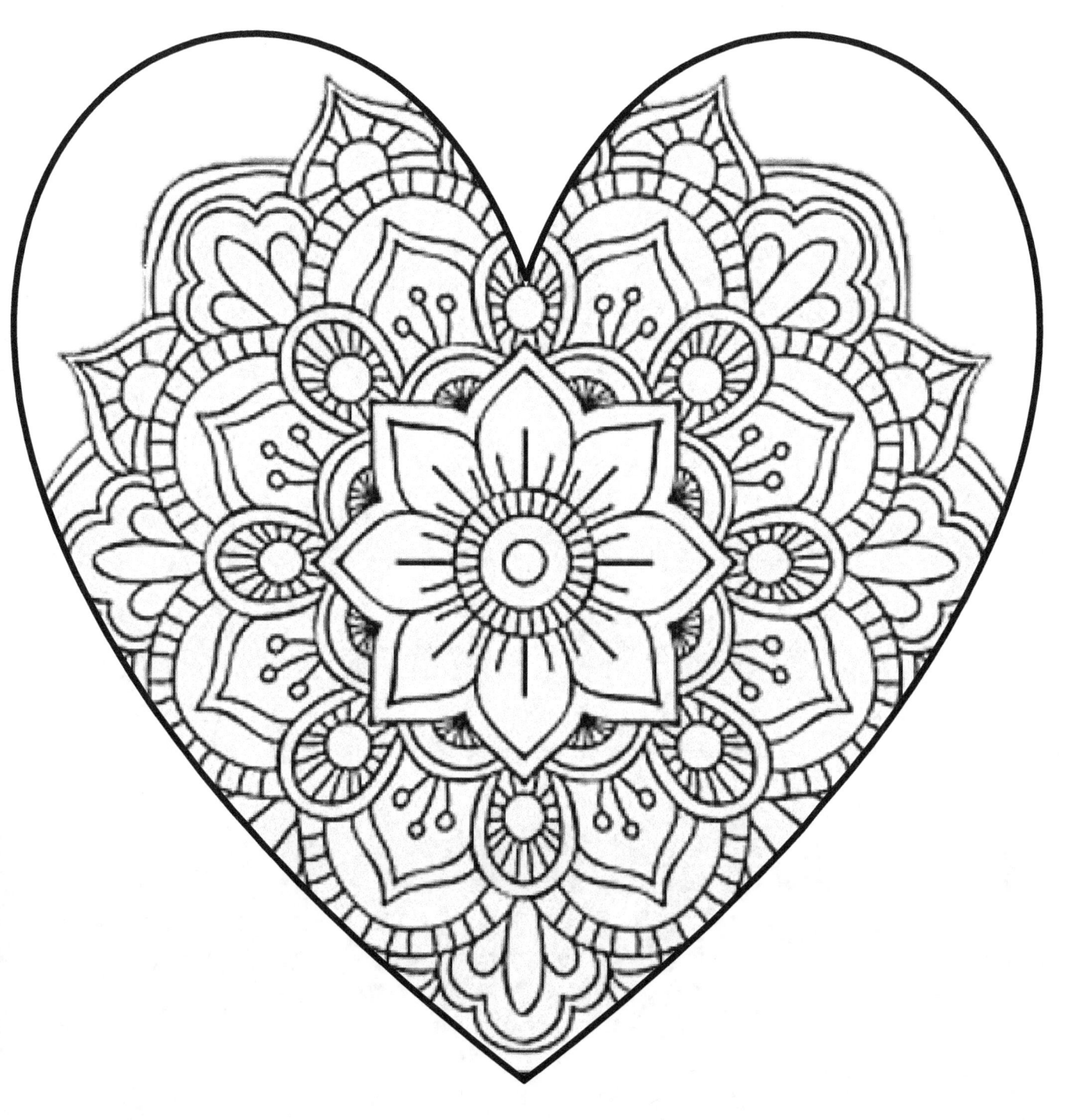

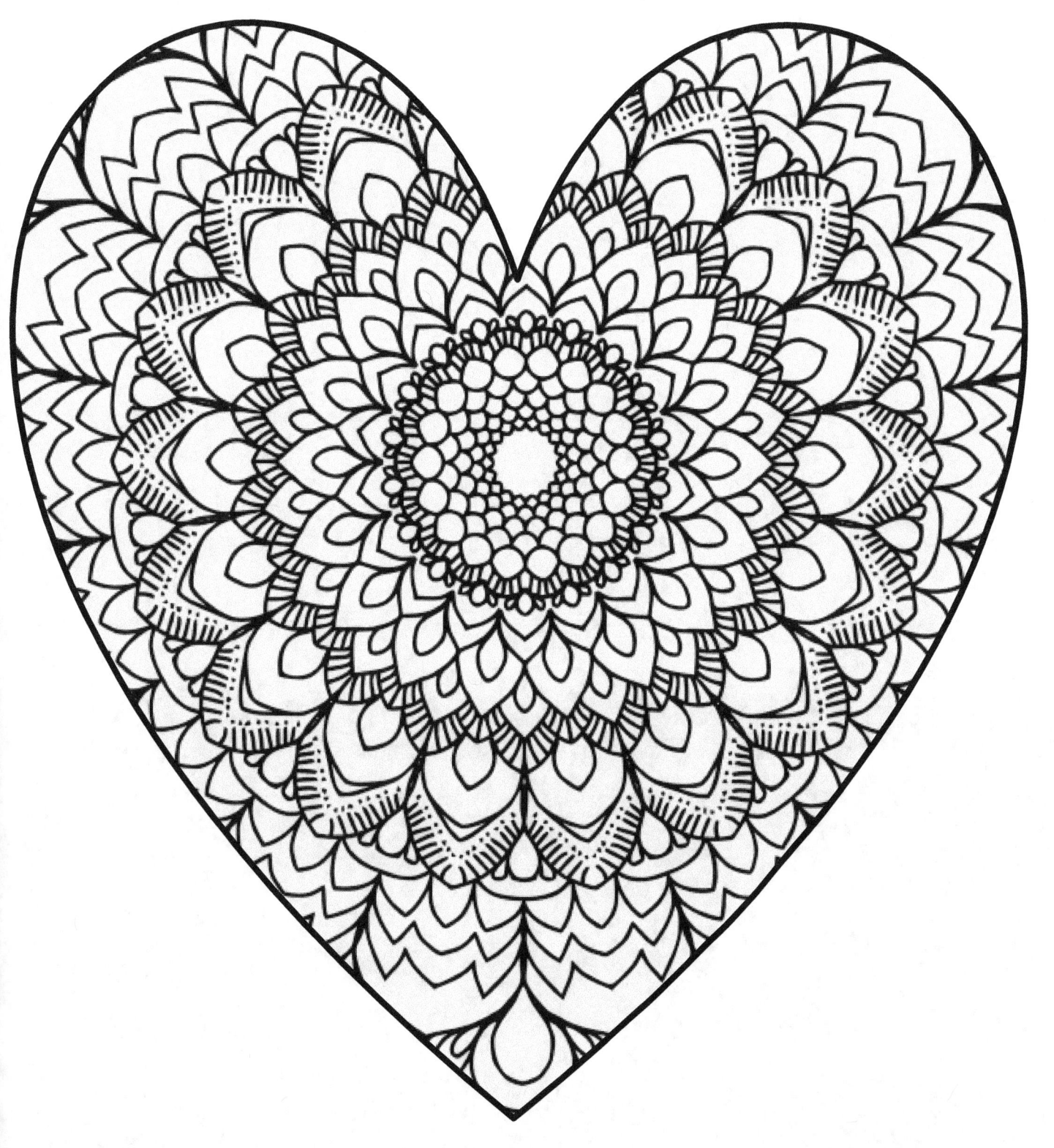

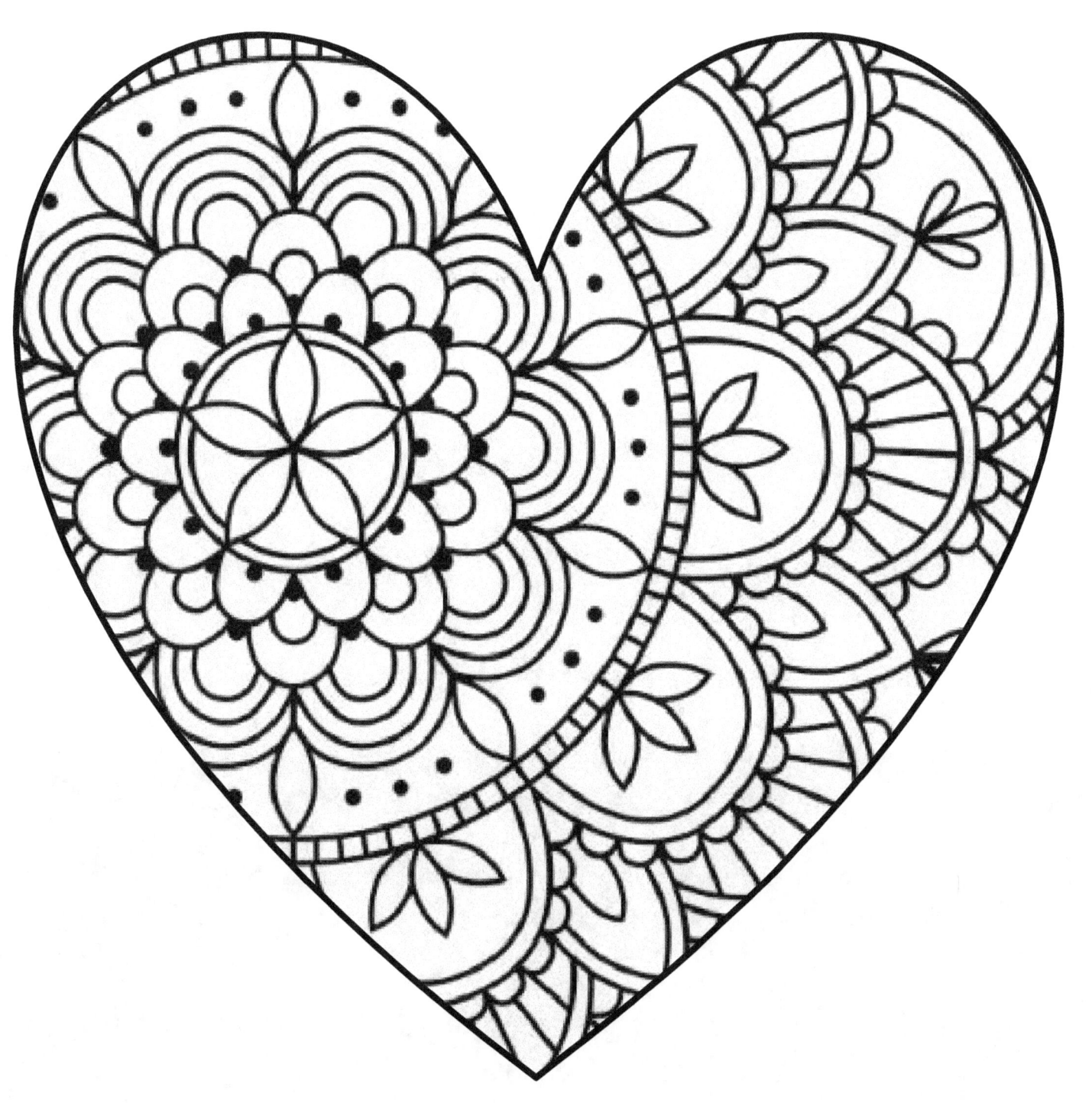

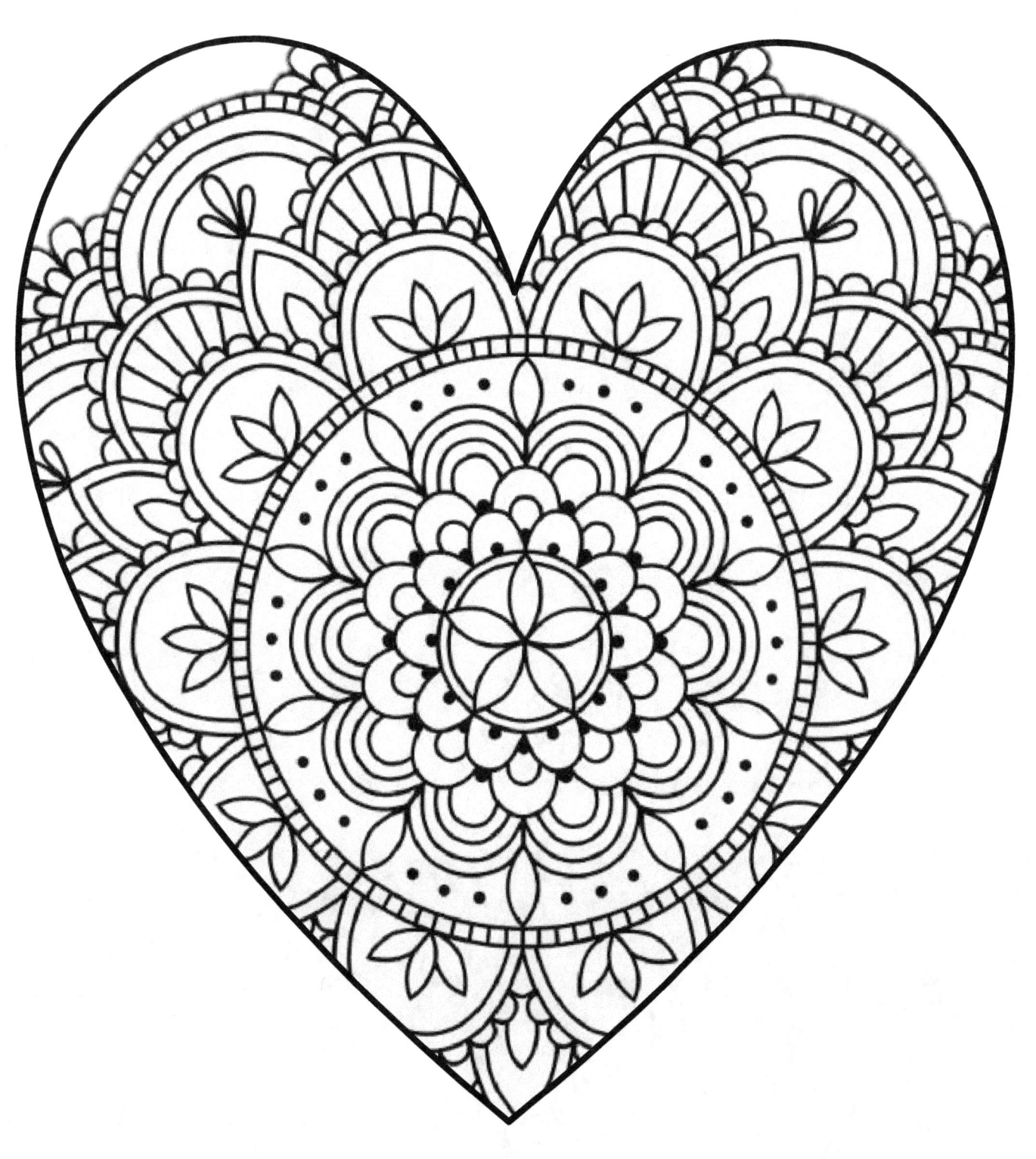

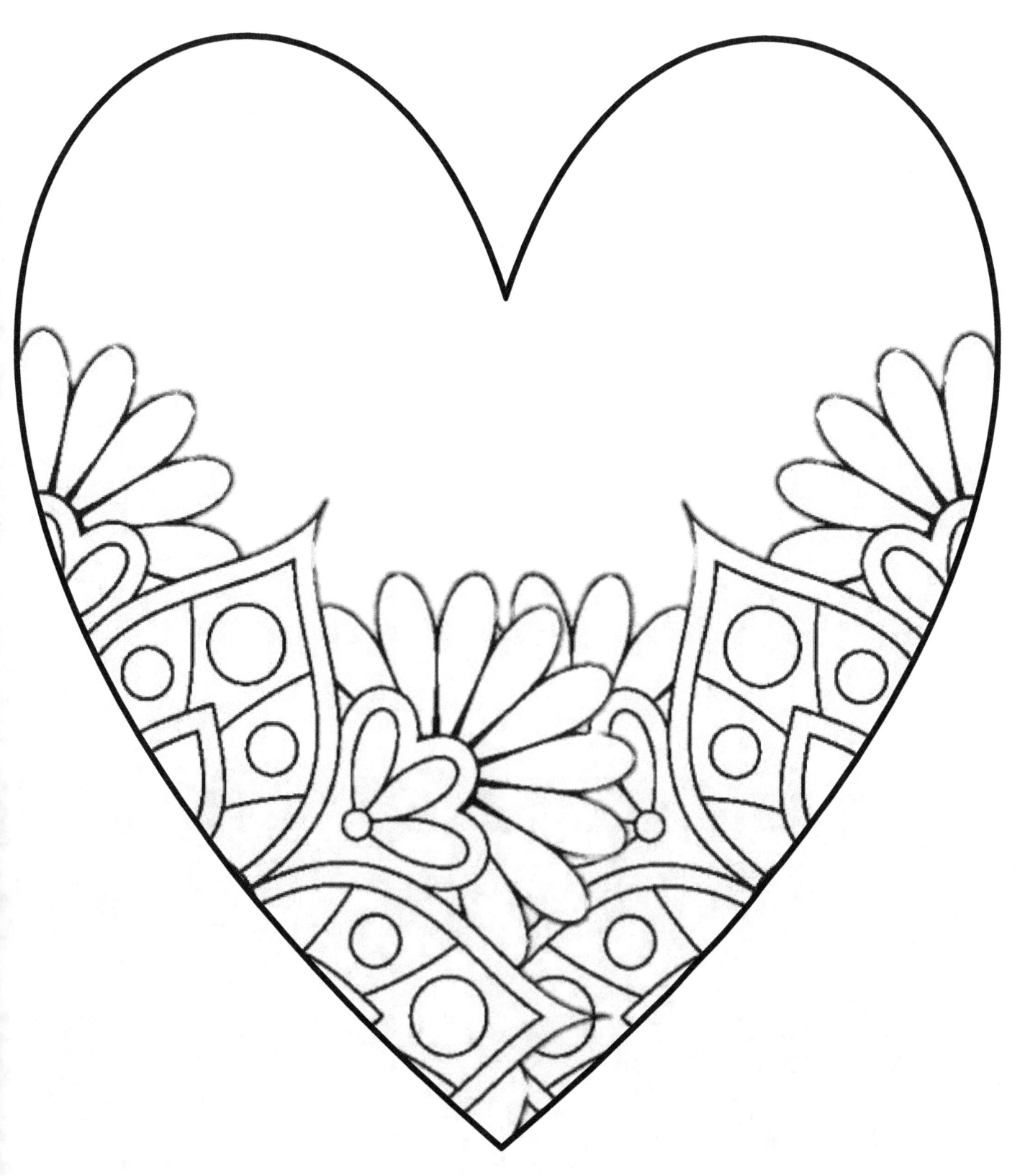

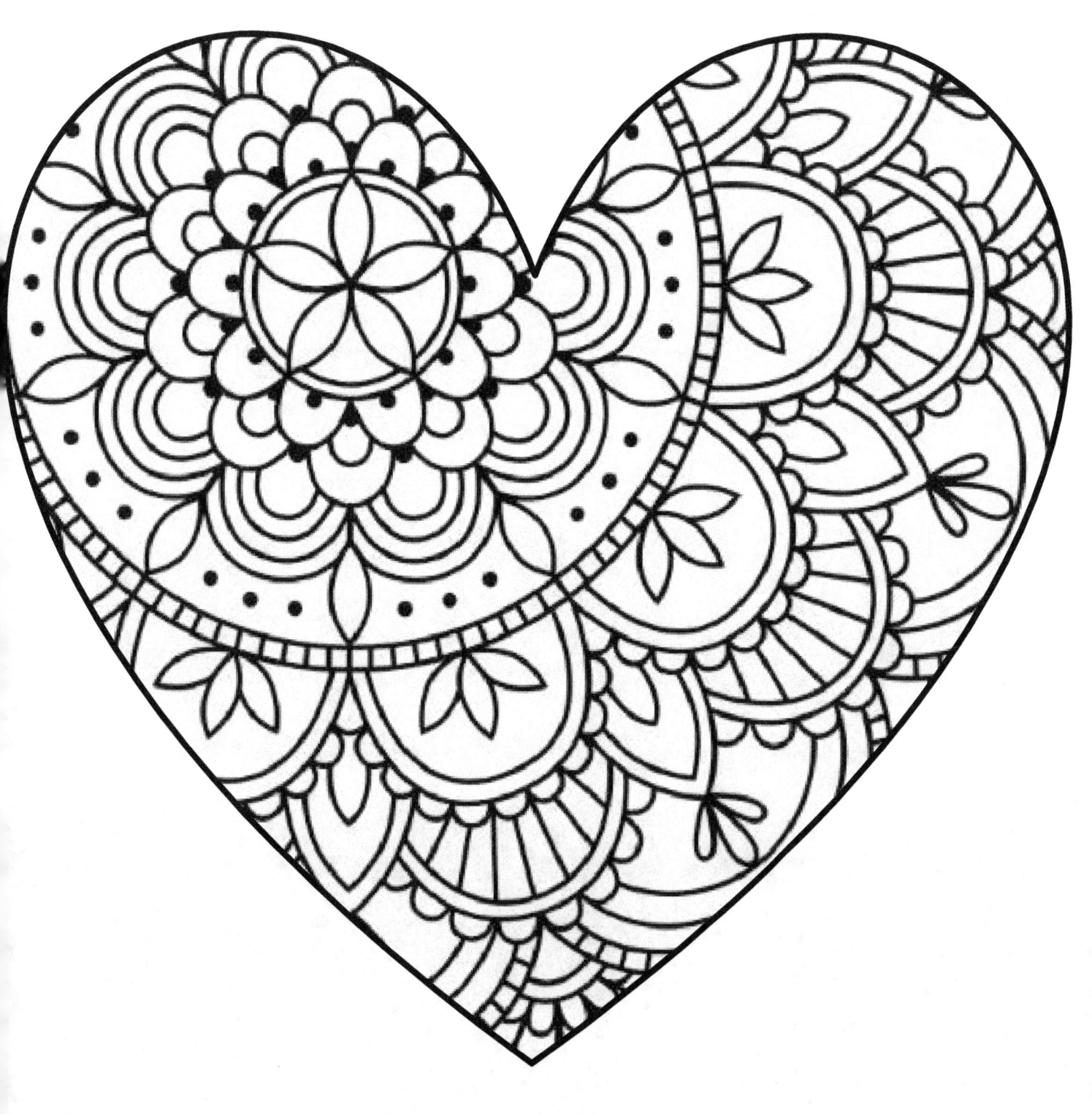

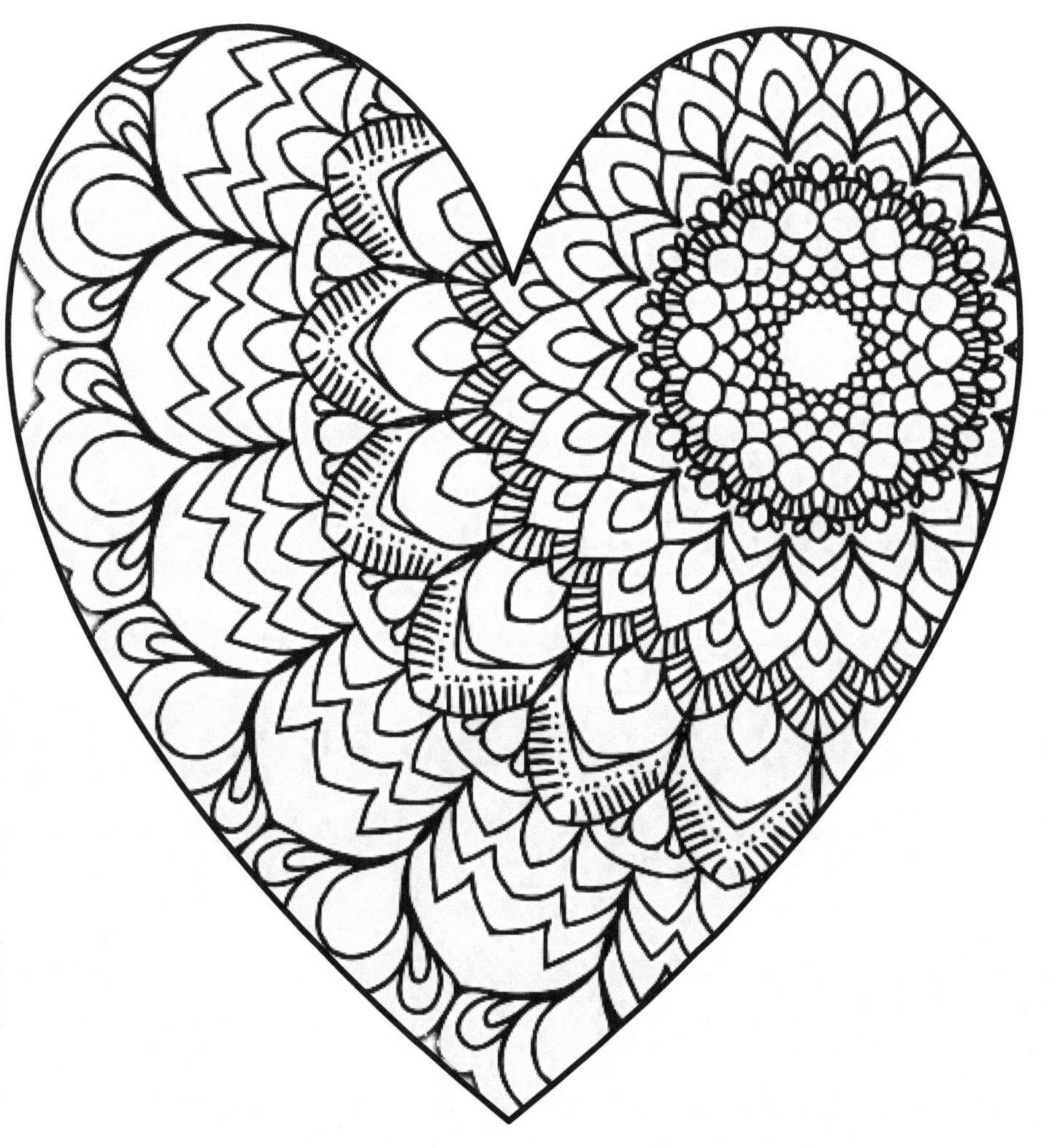

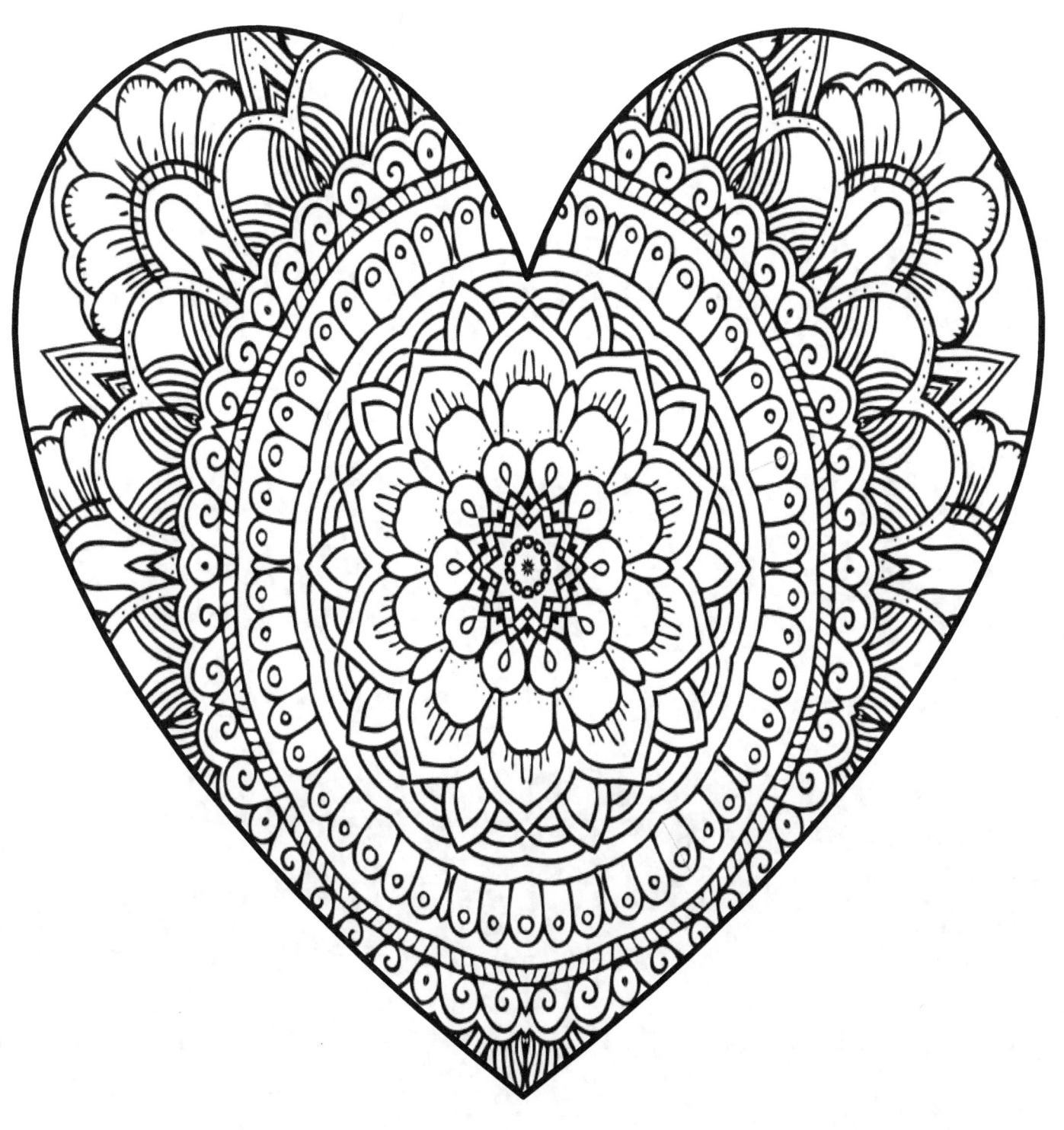

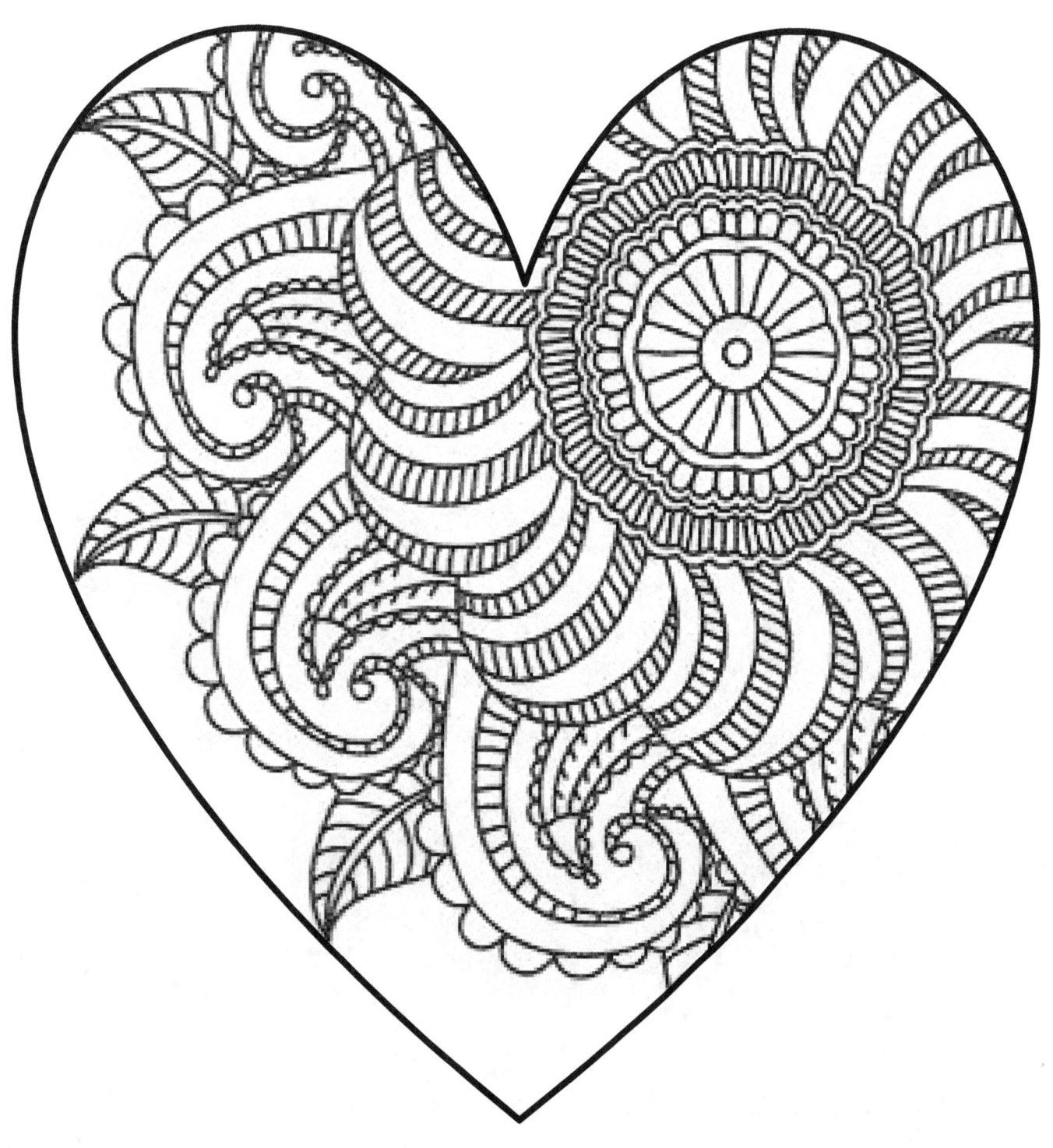

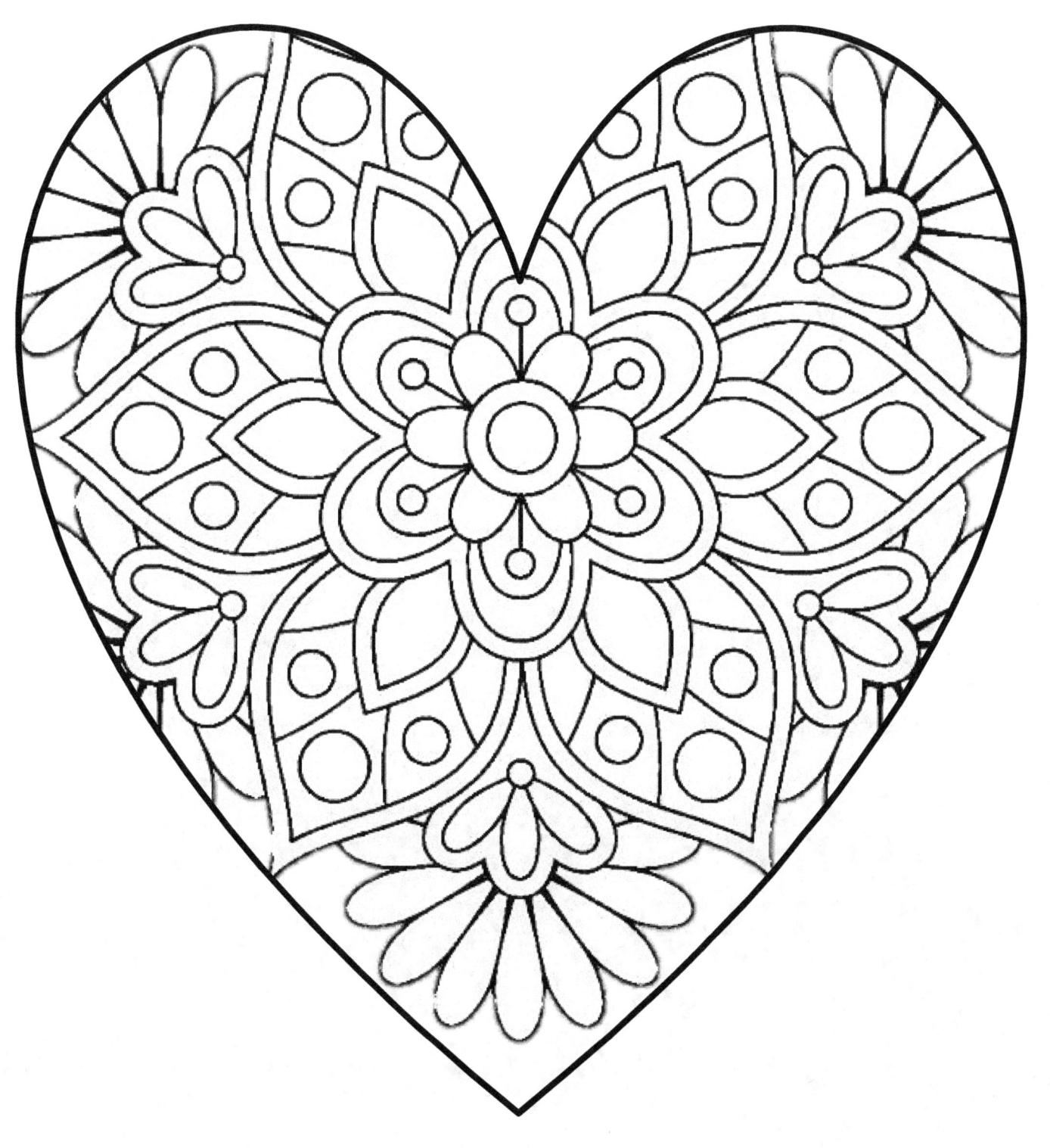

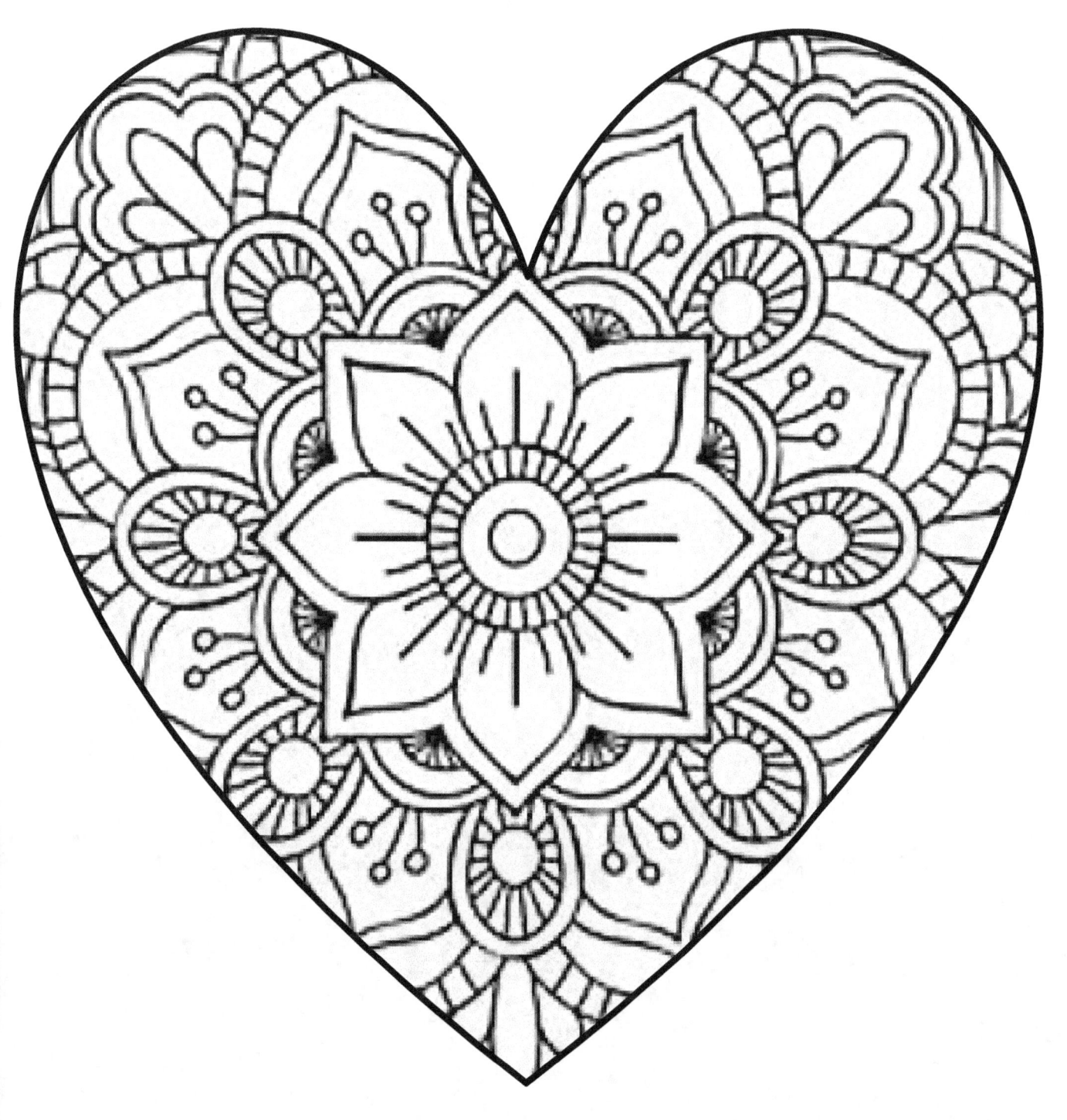

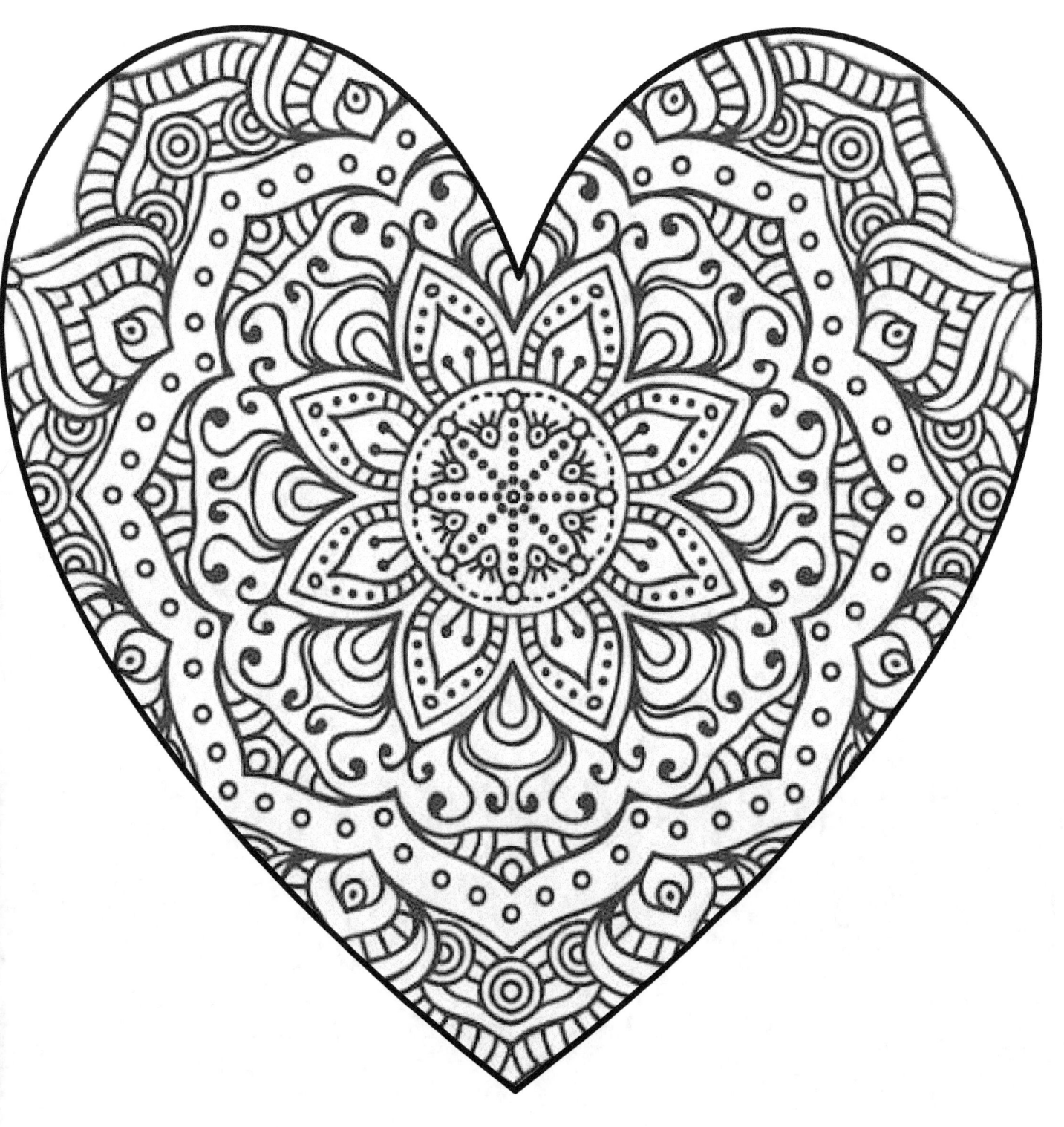

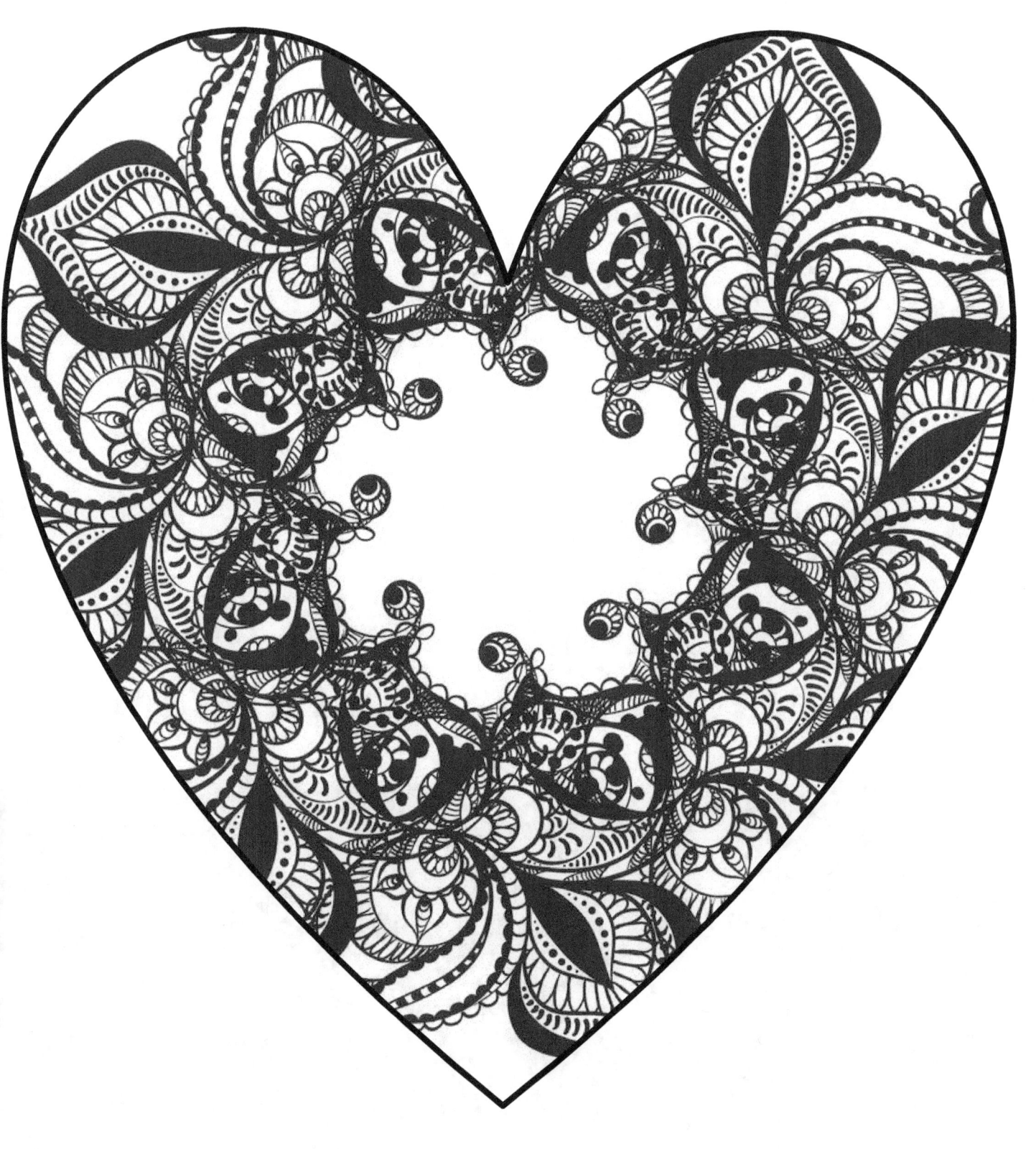

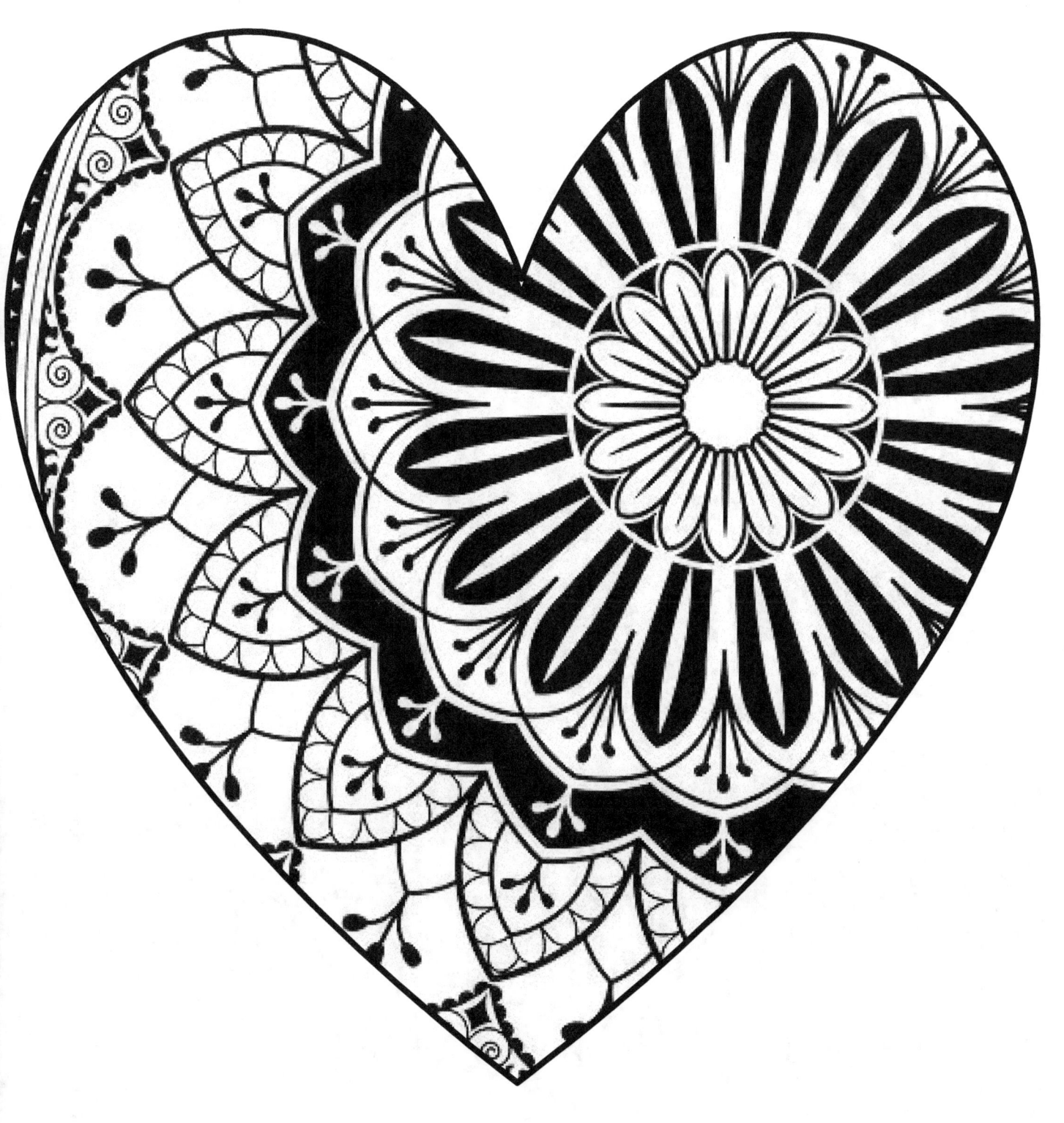

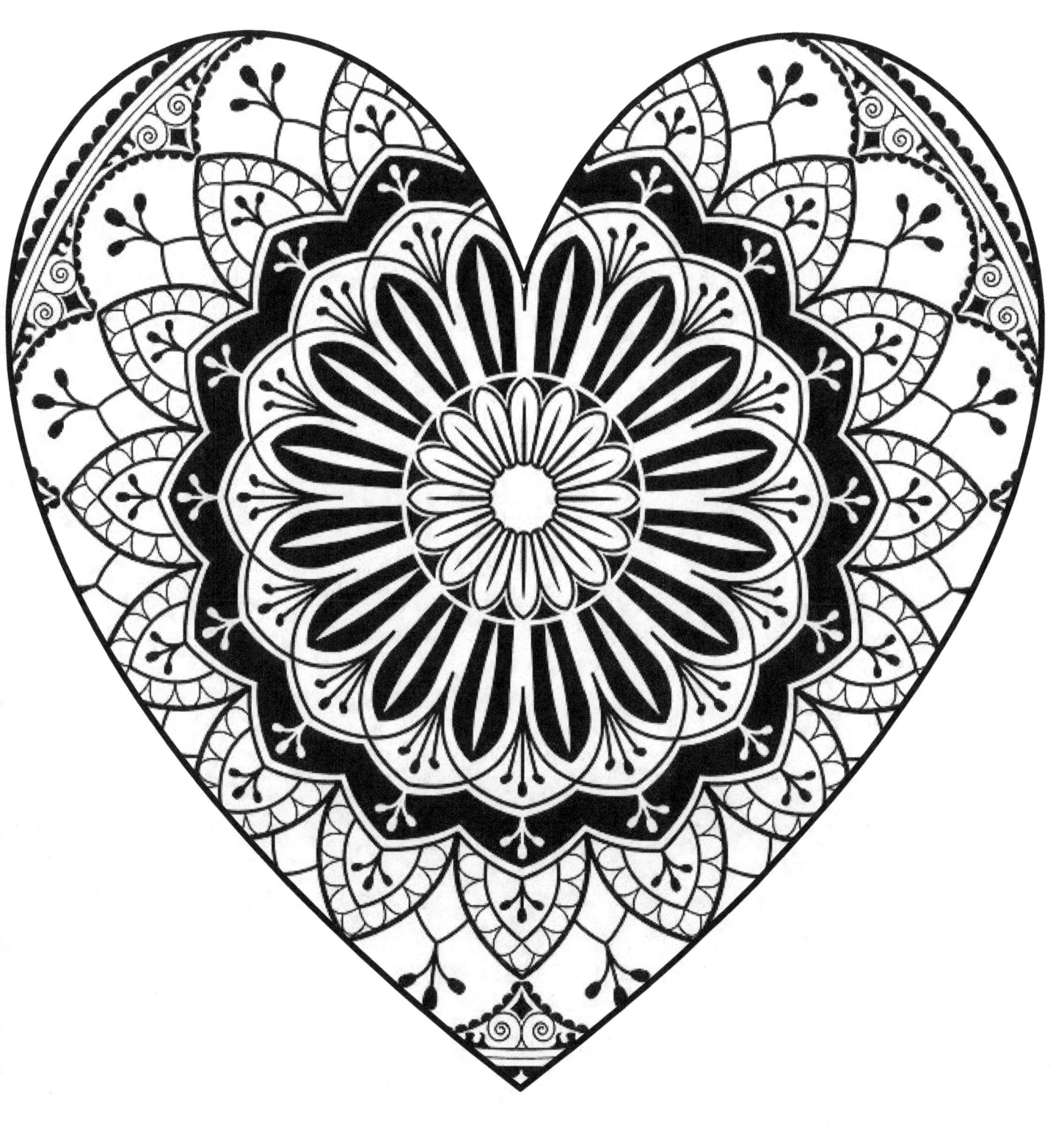

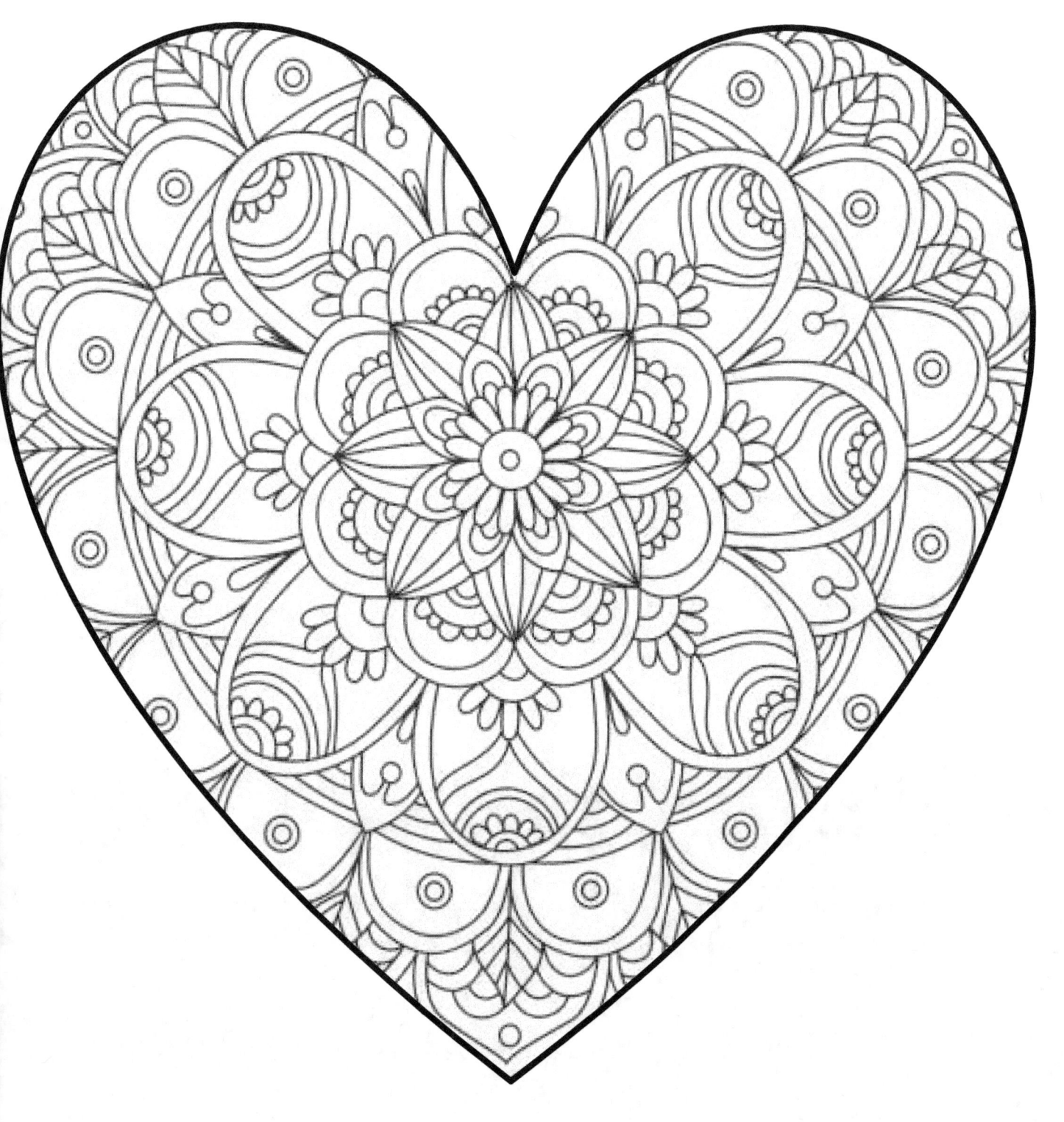

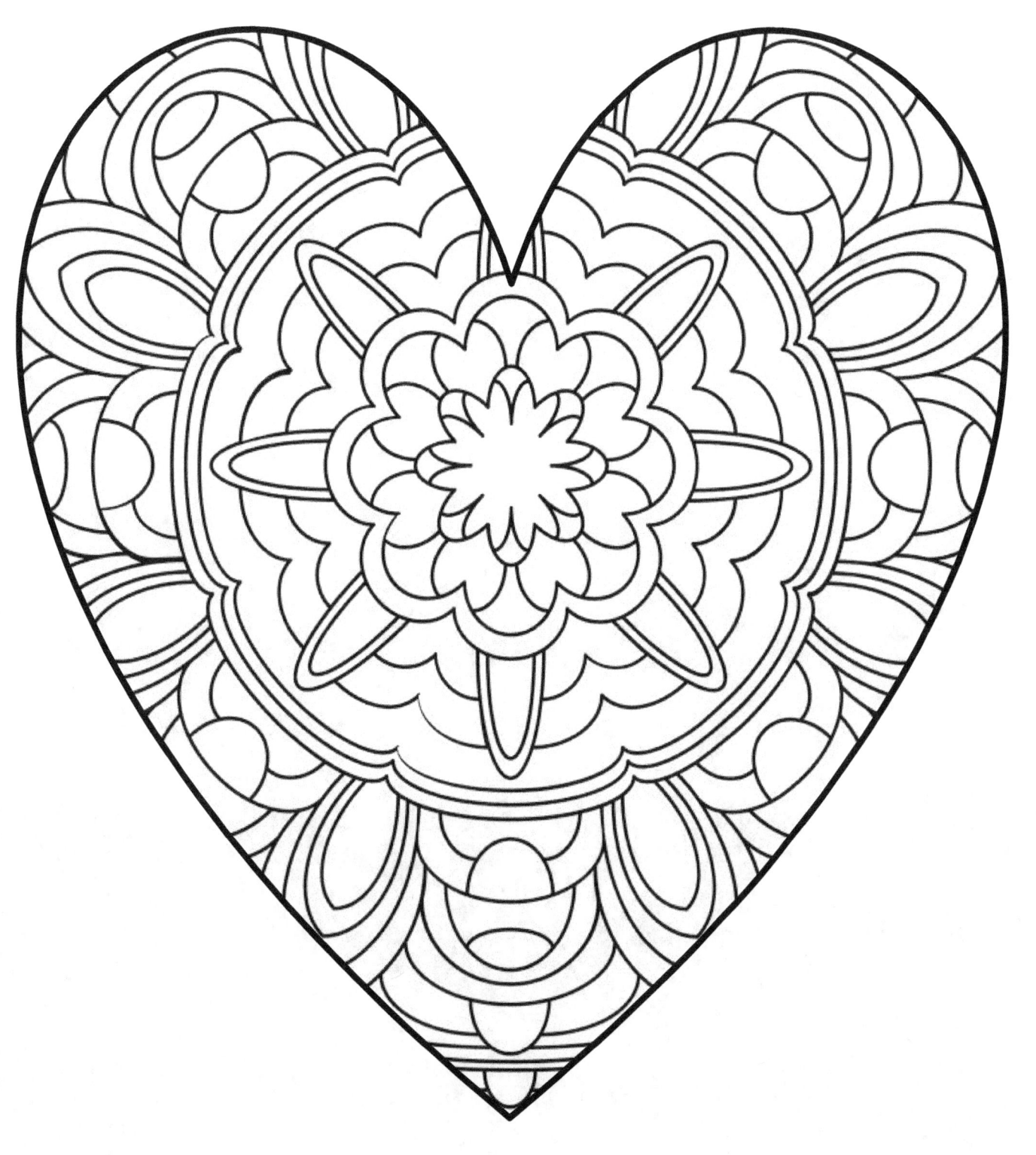

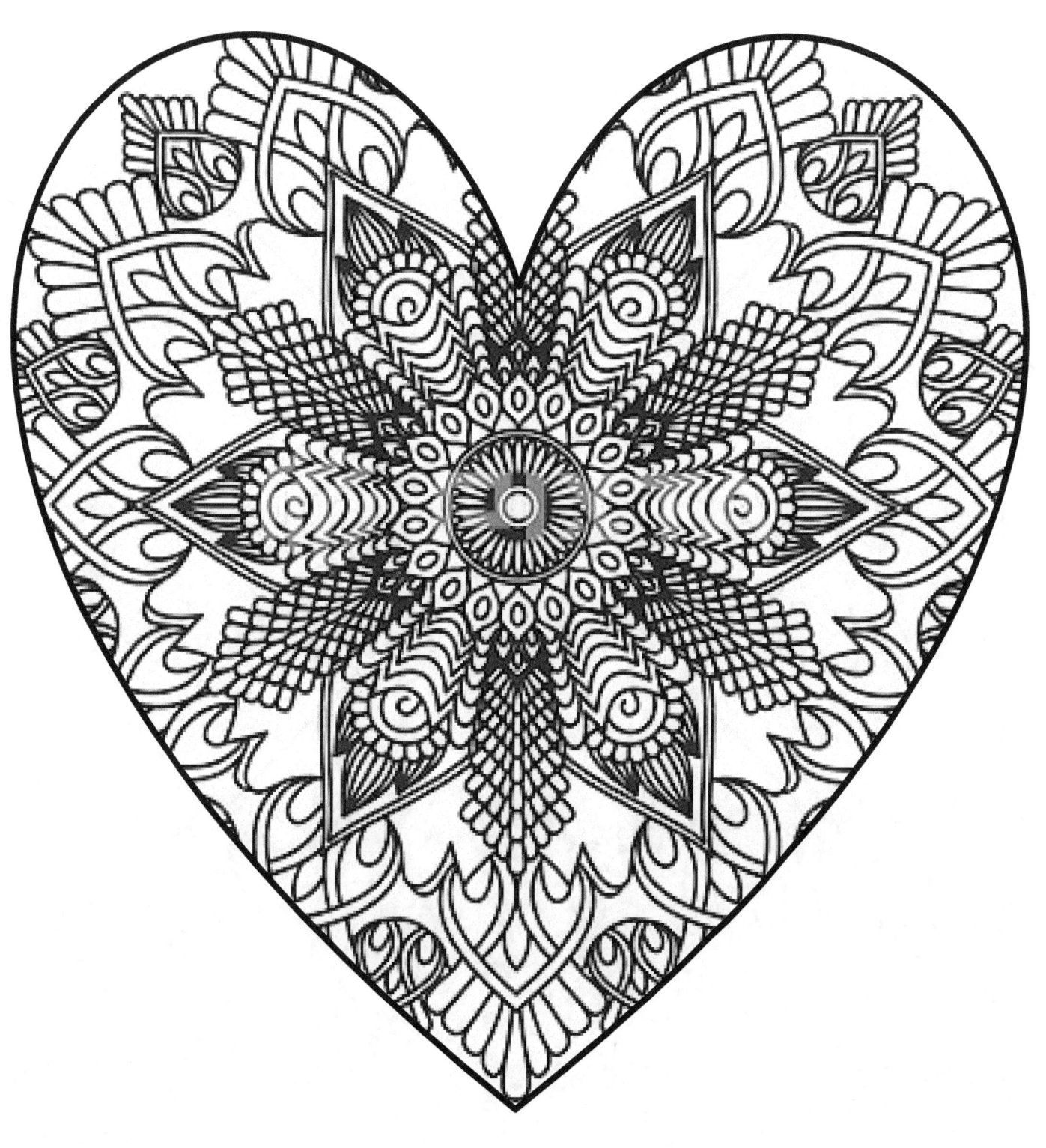

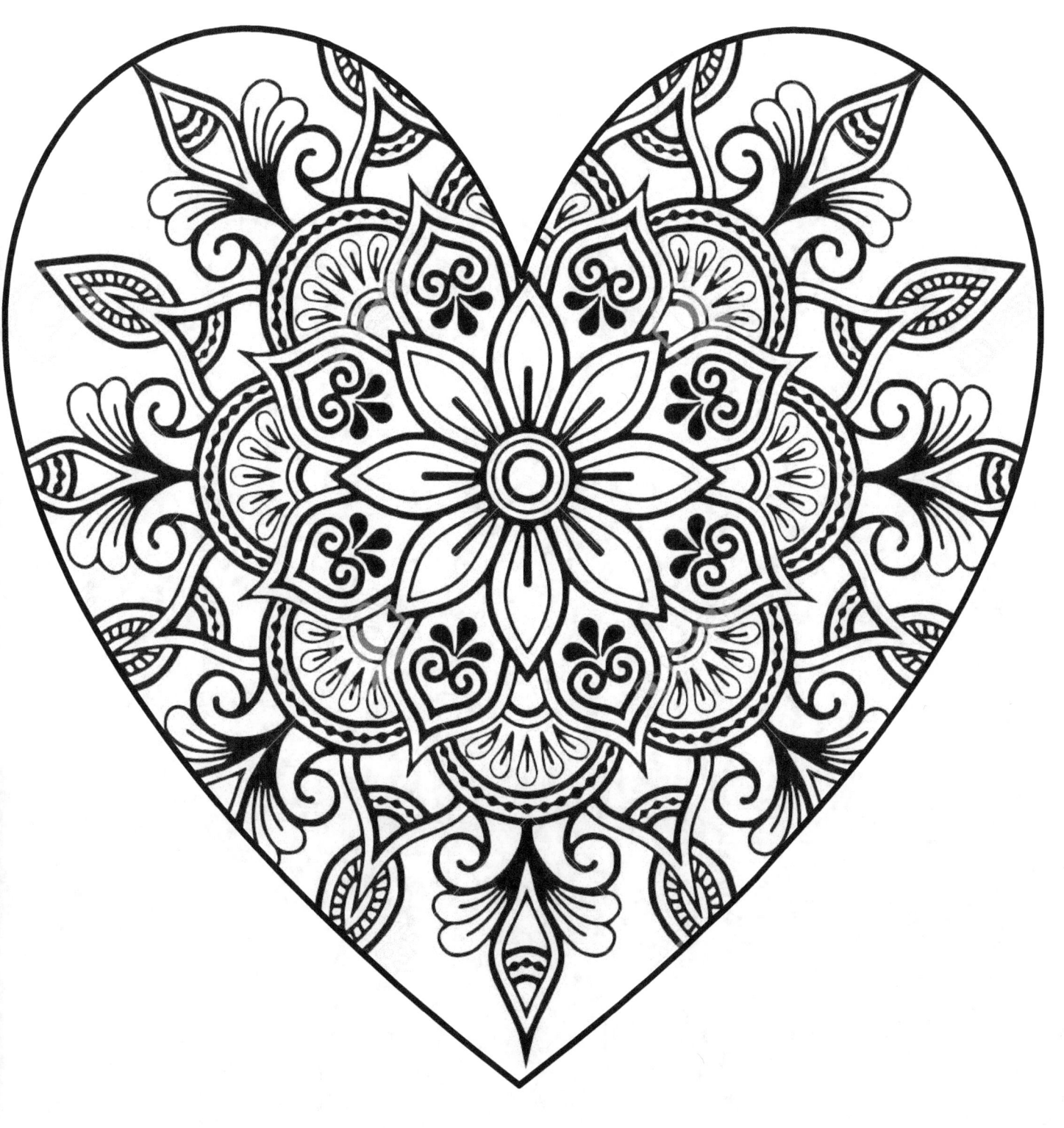

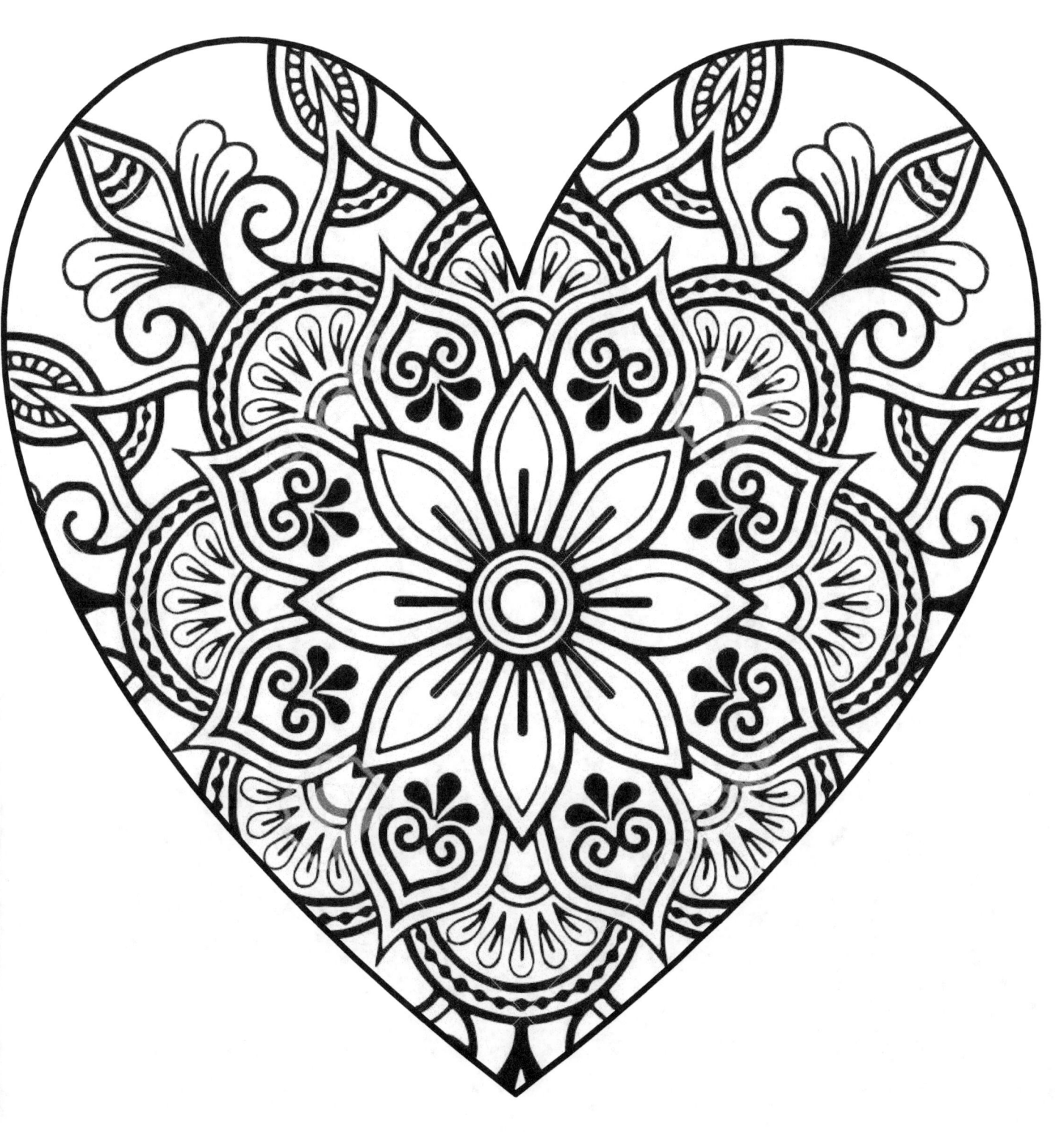

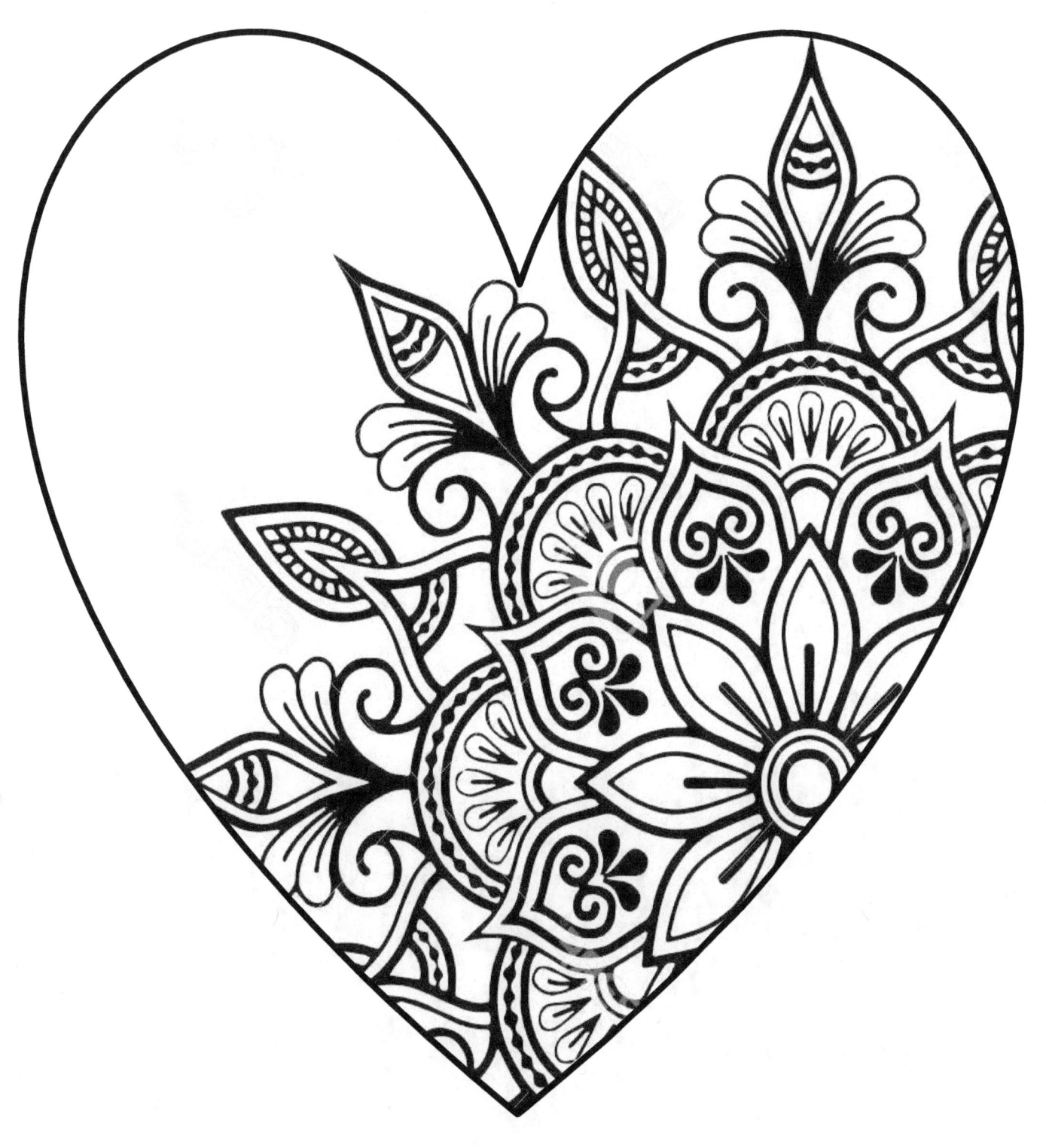

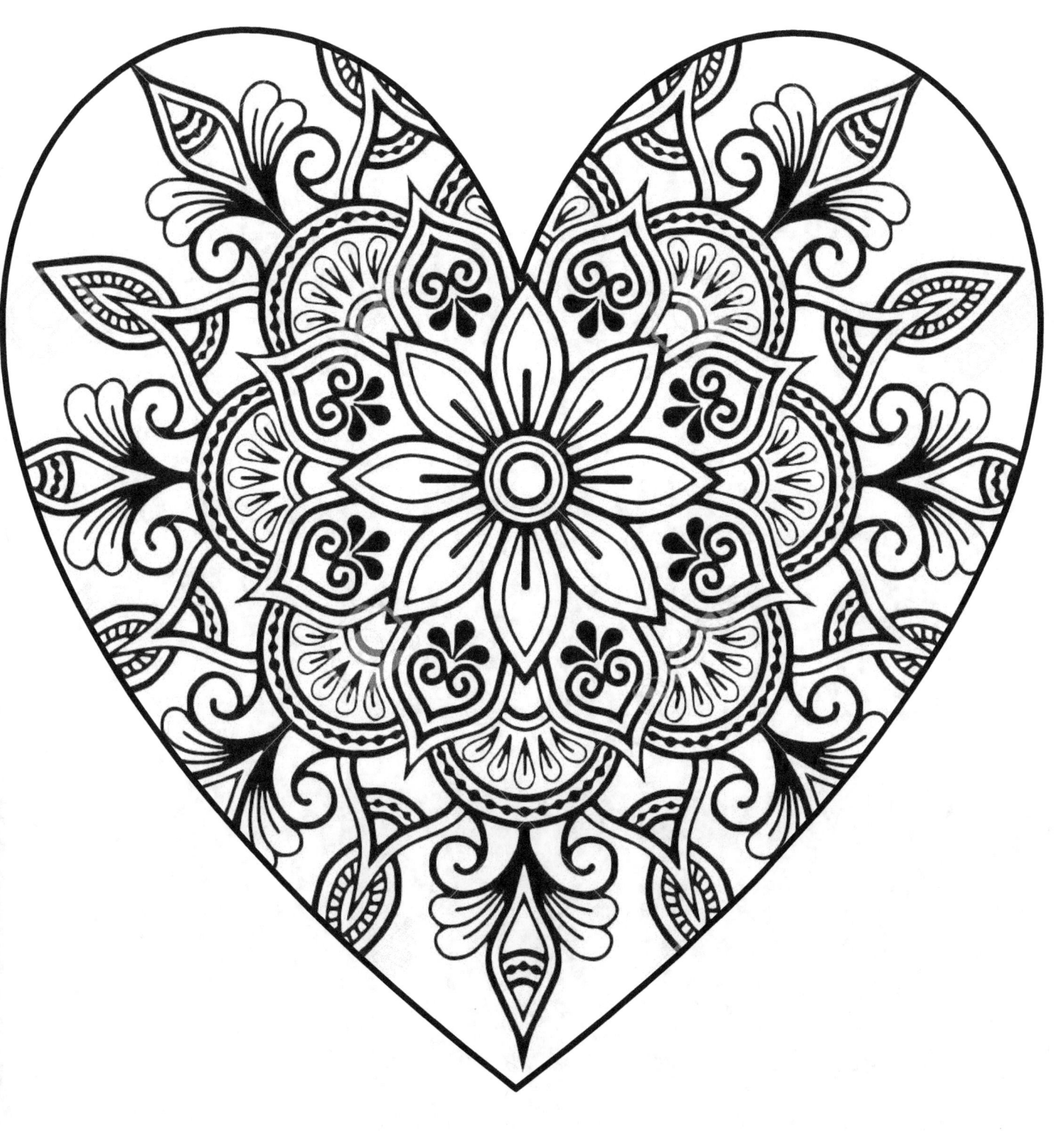

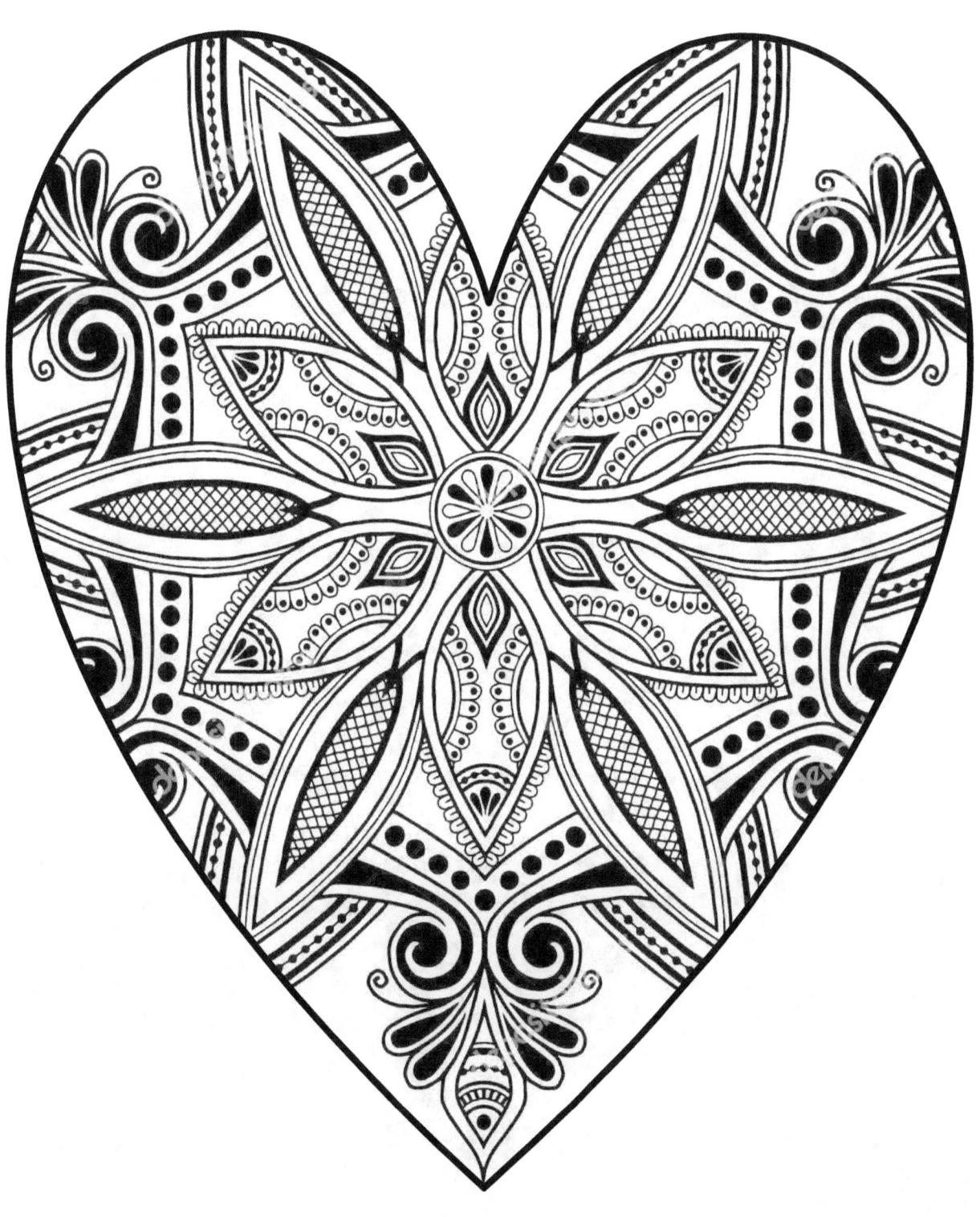

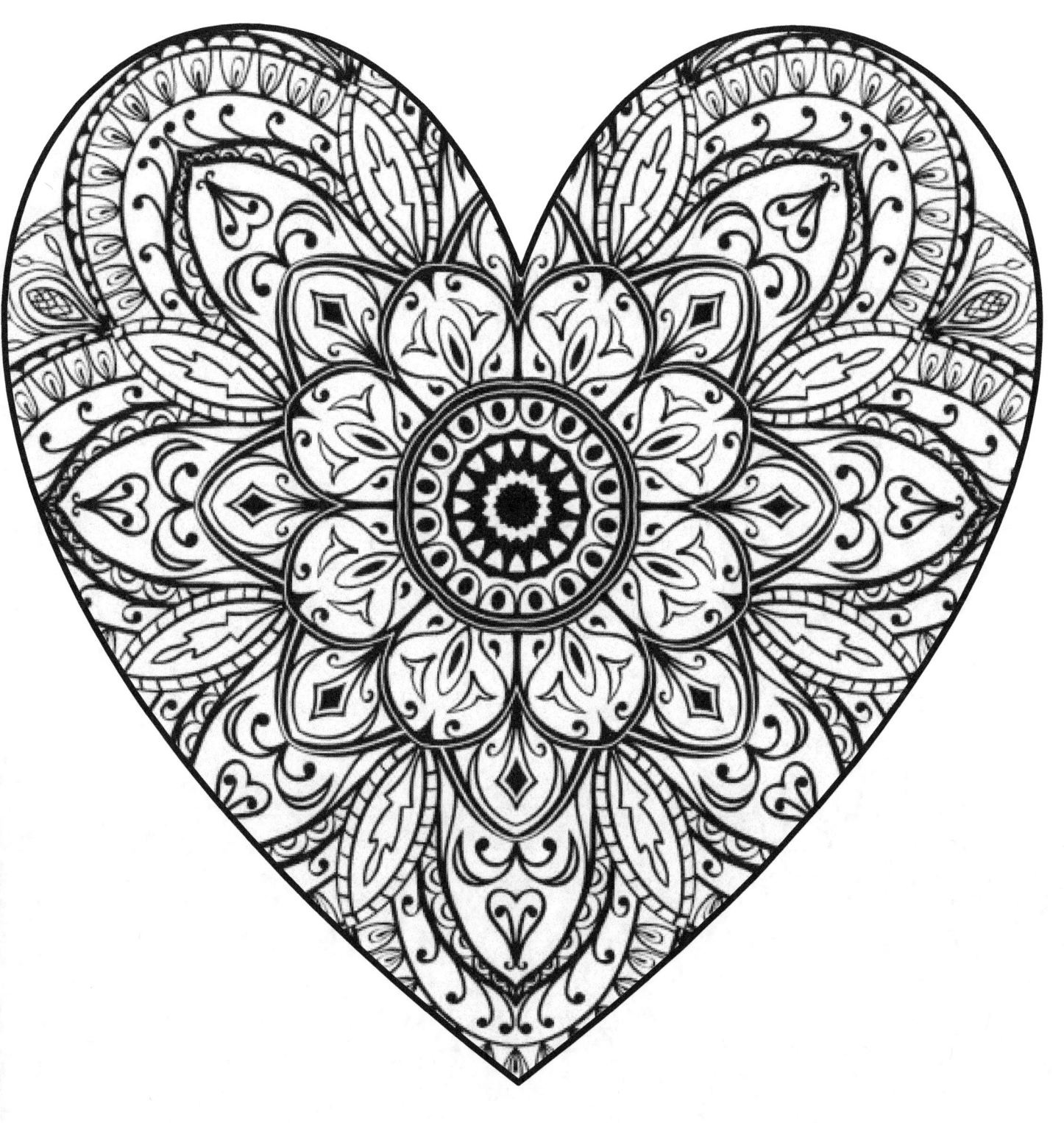

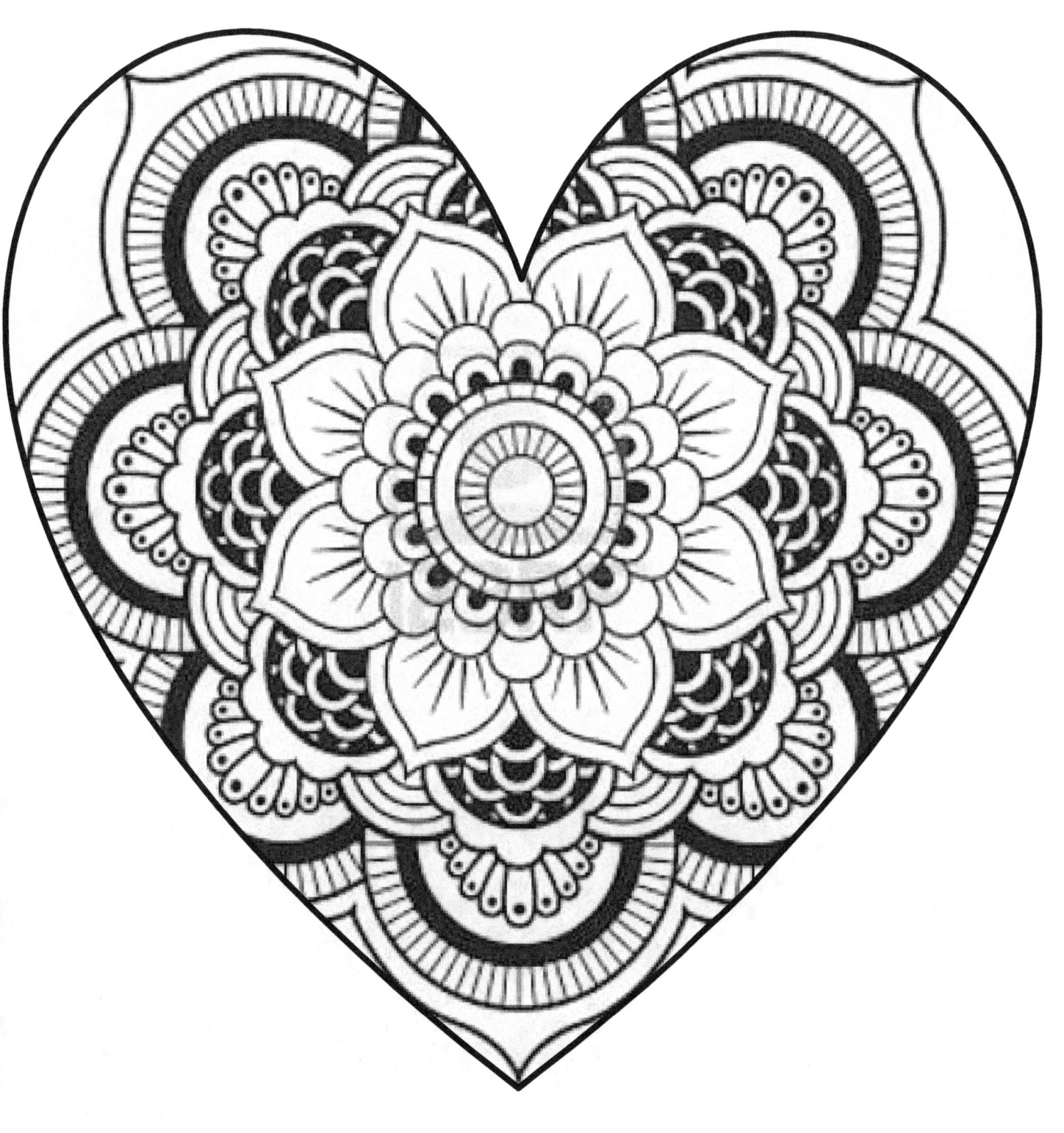

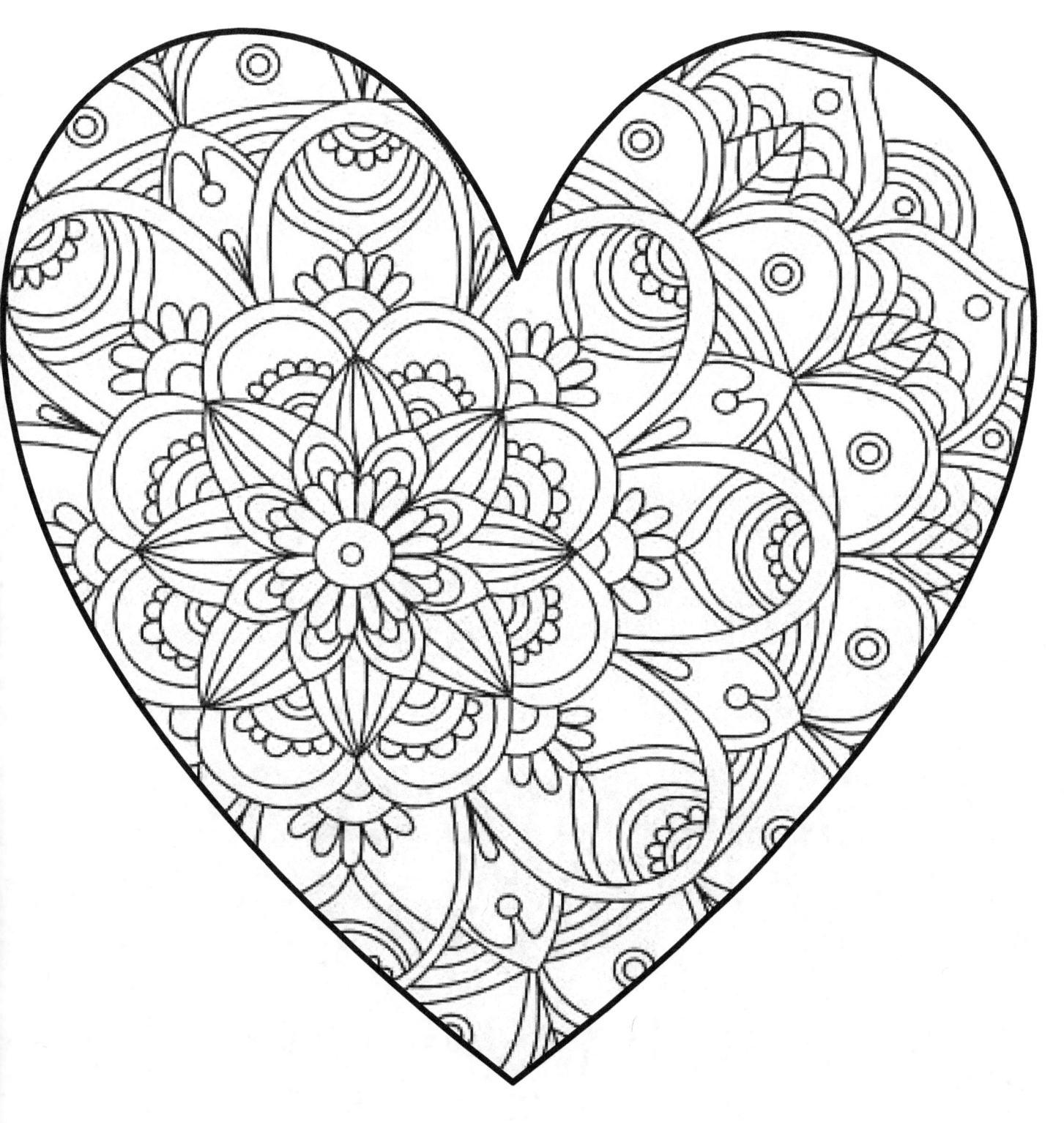

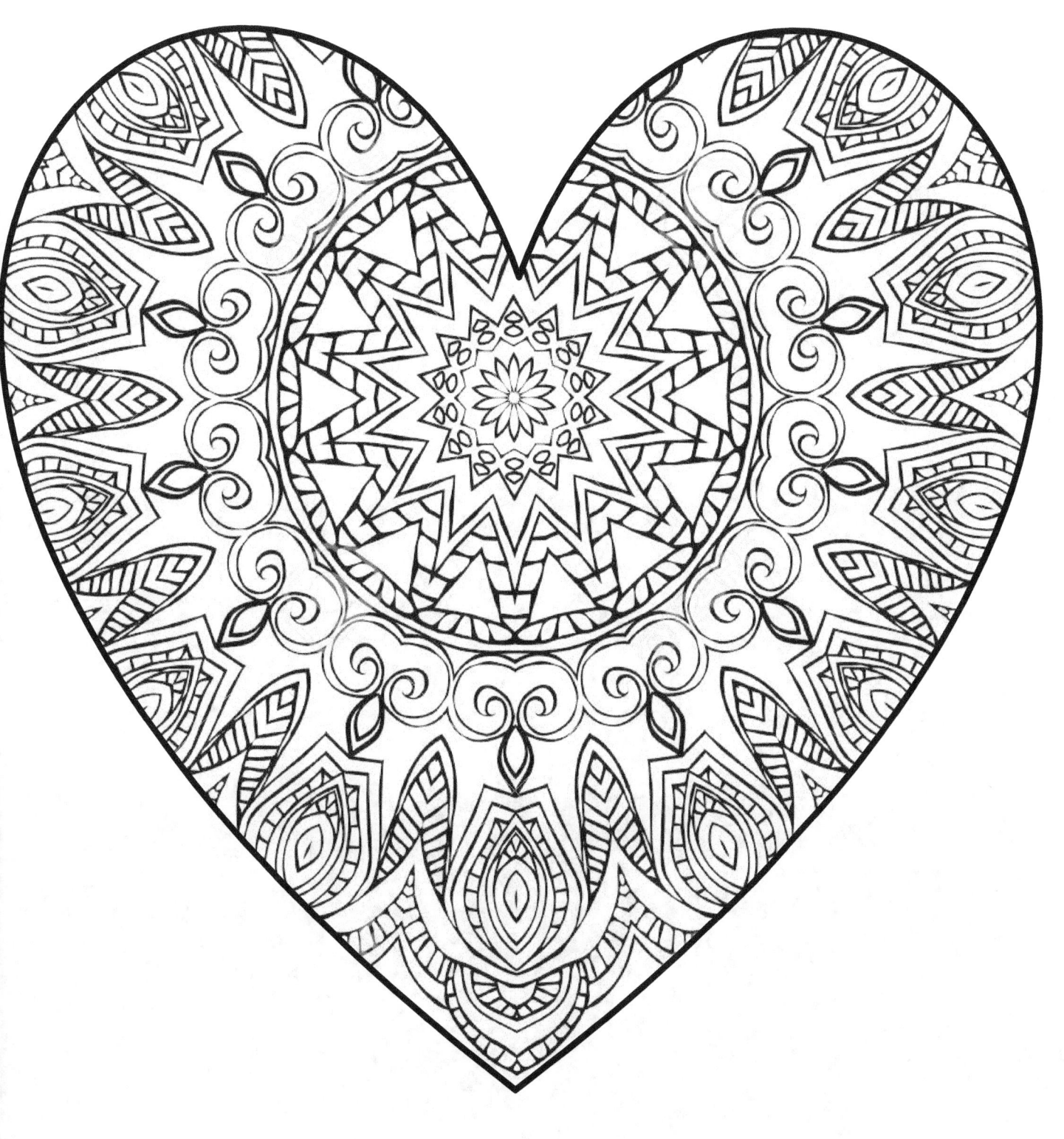

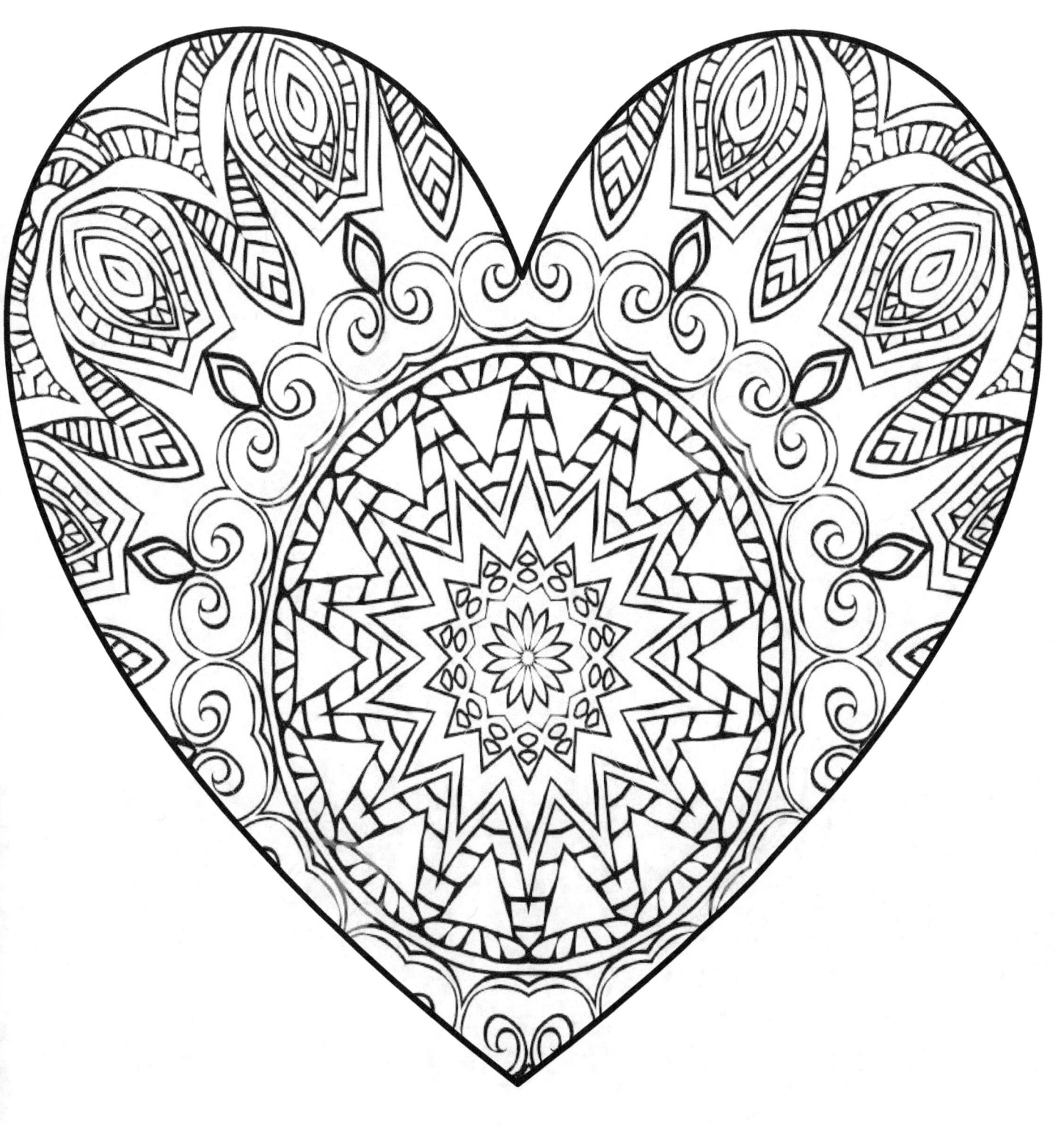

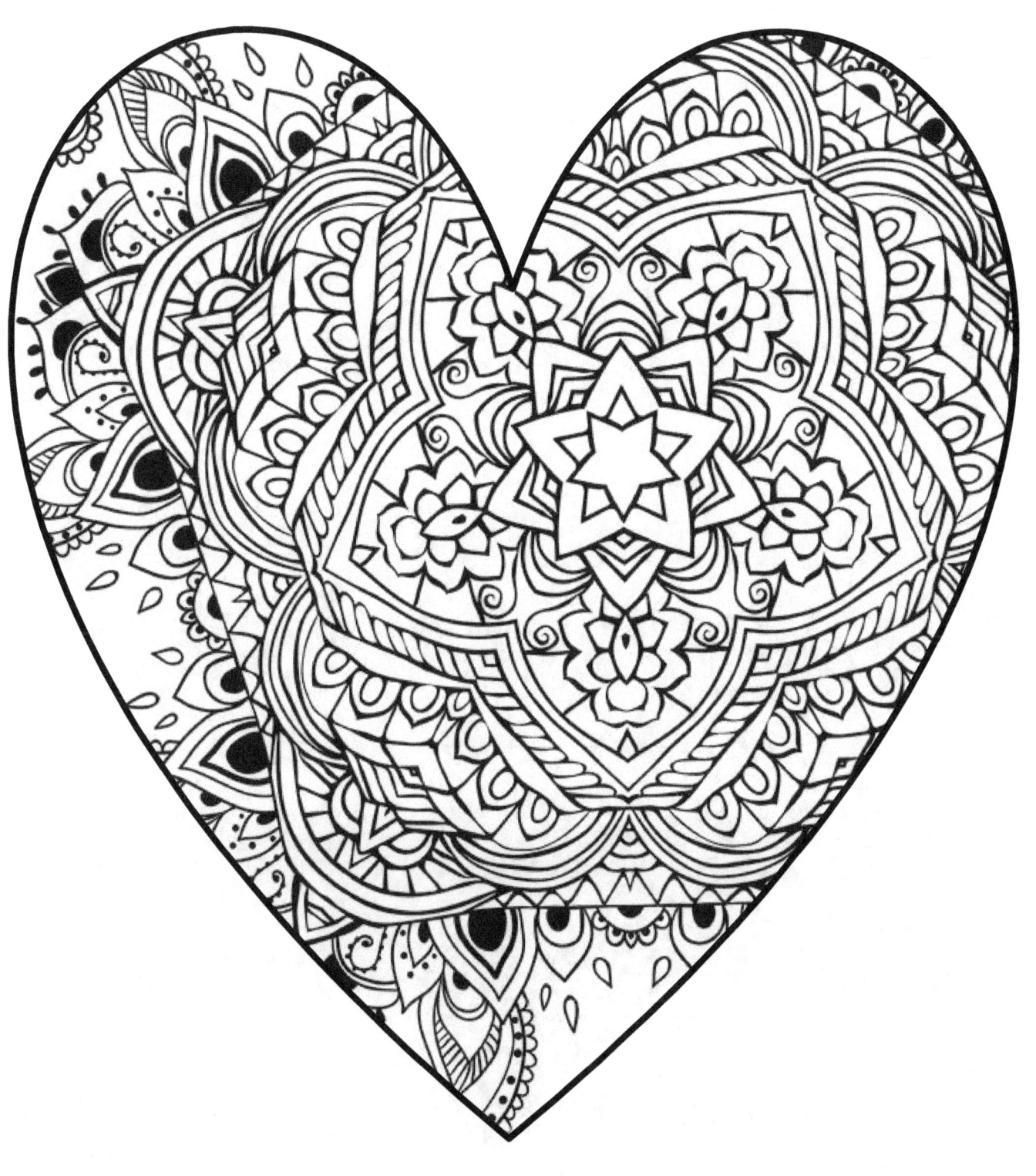

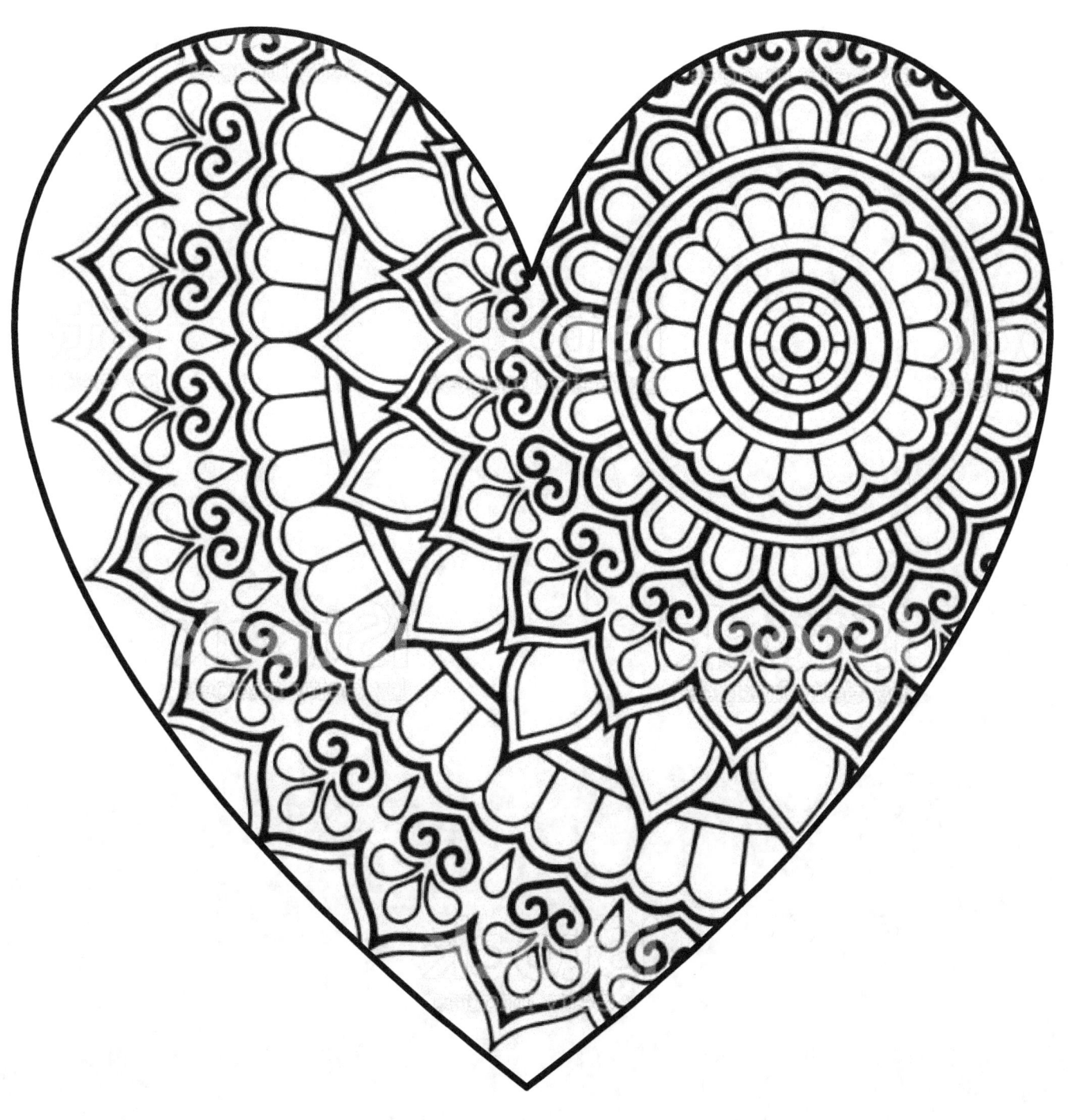

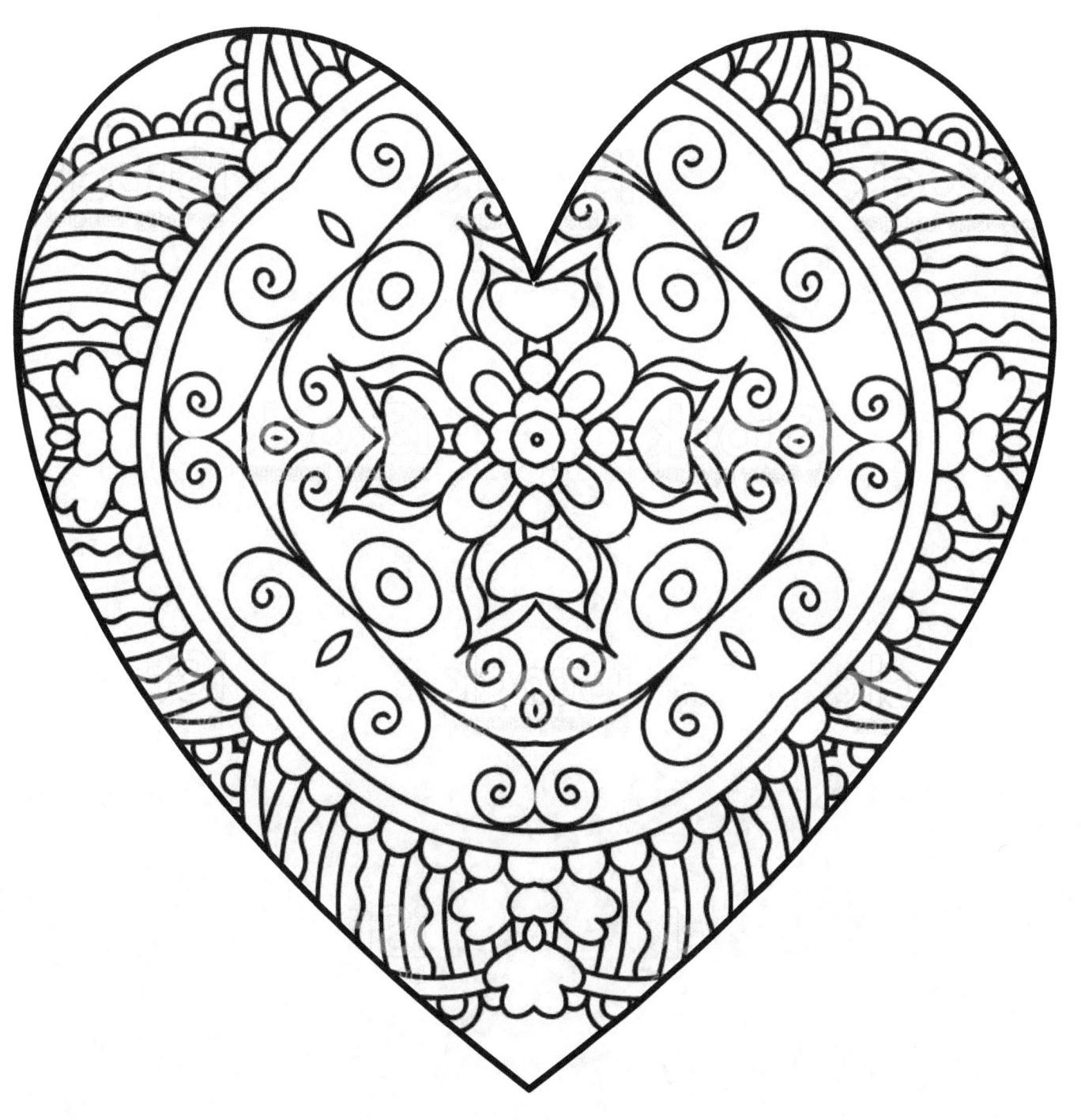

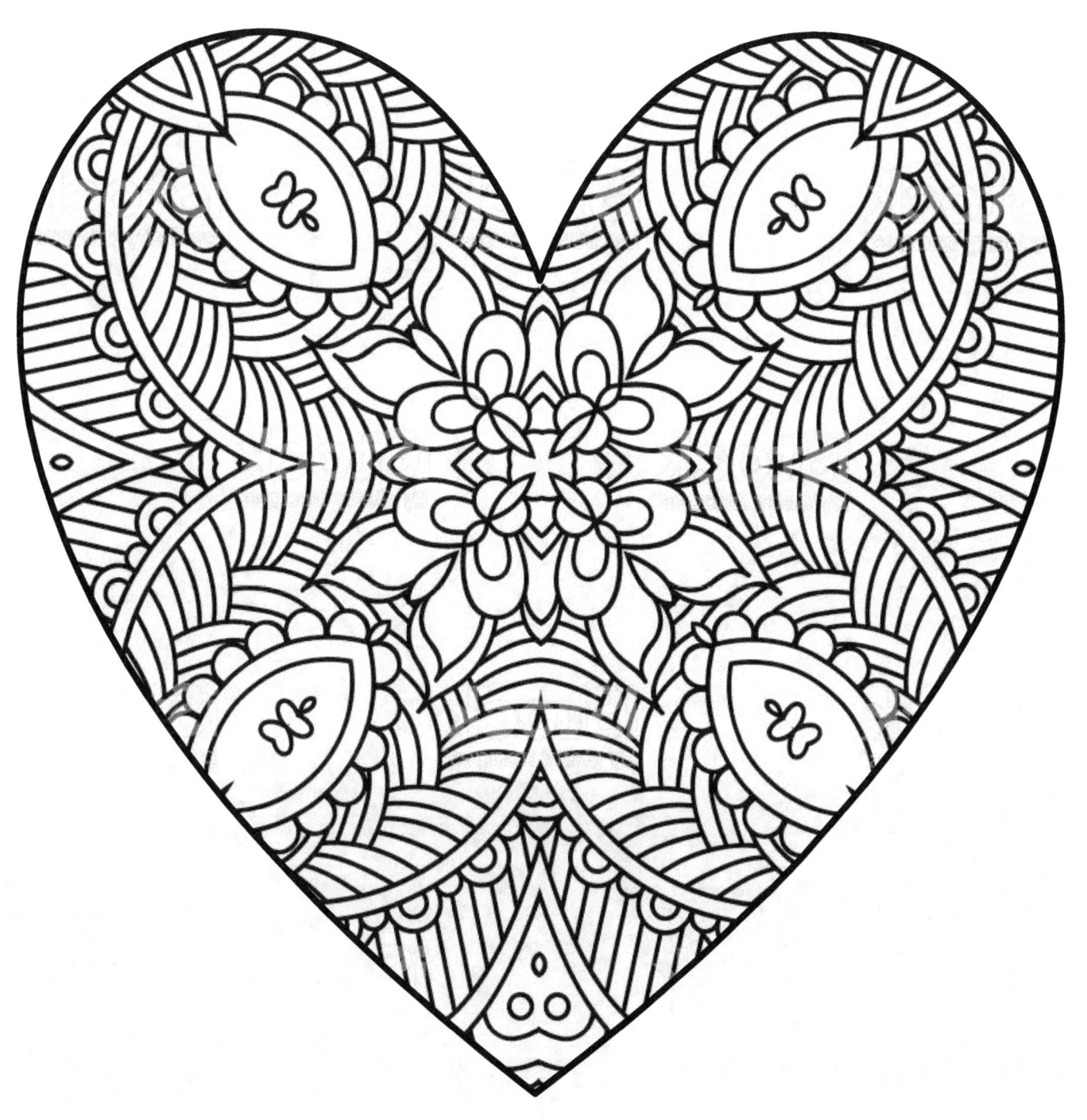

www.ingramcontent.com/pod-product-compliance
Lightning Source LLC
Chambersburg PA
CBHW081447220526
45466CB00008B/2538